D1562913

Lugenia Burns Hope

Black Southern Reformer

Lugenia Burns Hope

Black Southern Reformer

Jacqueline Anne Rouse

To Felix Armfield
may you continue
the tradition and
legacies of those who me
Sincerely,
Jacqueline A. Rouse
10/95

BROWN THRASHER BOOKS

The University of Georgia Press

Athens and London

© 1989 by the University of Georgia Press
Athens, Georgia 30602
All rights reserved

Designed by Kathi L. Dailey
Set in Mergenthaler Berkley Old Style and Benguiat
Typeset by The Composing Room of Michigan, Inc.
Printed and bound by Thomson-Shore
The paper in this book meets the guidelines for permanence
and durability of the Committee on Production Guidelines for
Book Longevity of the Council on Library Resources.

Printed in the United States of America

93 92 91 90 89 C 5 4 3 2 1

96 95 94 93 92 P 5 4 3 2 1

The Library of Congress has cataloged the hardback
edition of this work as follows:

Library of Congress Cataloging in Publication Data
Rouse, Jacqueline Anne.
  Lugenia Burns Hope, black southern reformer / Jacqueline
Anne Rouse.
    p. cm.
  Bibliography: p.
  Includes index.
  ISBN 0-8203-1082-4 (alk. paper)
  ISBN 0-8203-1464-1 (pbk.: alk. paper)
    1. Hope, Lugenia Burns. 2. Afro-Americans—Southern
States—Biography. 3. Social reformers—Southern States—
Biography. 4. Southern States—History—1865–1951. I. Title.
E185.97.H717R68   1989
973'.0496073024—dc19
[B]   88-17521
                                                              CIP

British Library Cataloging in Publication Data available

To my mother, Mrs. Fannie T. Rouse

To the memory of my father, Mr. John H. Rouse

And to all my kindred spirits.

Contents

Acknowledgments

This work is a collective effort from numerous sources of motivation, encouragement, and strength. Support has come from persons who encouraged me, the individual, and from those who championed the preservation and resurrection of Black women's lives and activism. Thus the publication of this manuscript materialized from the hopes, the well wishes, and the prayers of many.

My dissertation advisor at Emory University, Darlene Roth, was always convinced that the materials were available and the urgency was great to write this biography. She believed that this work would help fill a major void in southern women's history. The project was made possible by Alton Hornsby, Jr., editor of the John and Lugenia Burns Hope Papers. Professor Hornsby, a member of my dissertation committee, permitted the perusal of these papers prior to their availability to the public.

Members of the Hopes and Burnses have given much assistance and support. Lugenia Burns Hope's two sons shared recollections of their parents and their years at Morehouse College. Edward Hope wrote a lengthy document in response to my numerous questions. John Hope II and Elise Hope shared personal anecdotes and incidents that brought Hope to life. Anna Elder, a cousin, assisted in identifying family photographs in the Emma and Lloyd Lewis Collection at the University of Illinois, Chicago Circle. But Lugenia Hope's grandniece, Heneritha Meredith, proved the family historian. Via lengthy telephone conversations and several onsite visits, she rescued me often by filling in the gaps in the Burns's history, by identifying the photographs in the Lewis Collection, and by letting me know of other living family members, especially Jeanette Garrett, Lugenia's grandniece.

The staffs of several libraries and collections were helpful. I am grateful to the Special Collection and Archives, Robert Woodruff Library, Atlanta University Center; Special Collections, University Library, University of Illinois at Chicago Circle; Moorland Spingarn Research Center, Howard University; Manuscript Division, Library of Congress; Archives, Tuskegee Institute; and the Reference and Special Collection, Robert Woodruff Library, Emory University. I thank director John Kinnard, Louise Hutchinson, and Gail Lowe of the Anacostia Neighborhood Museum, Smithsonian Institution, for their assistance in locating materials and for permission to peruse the Marion C. Hope Papers during the summer of 1982.

This manuscript was financially assisted by travel and research grants from the Strengthening the Humanities Summer Program of the United Negro College Fund and from the Mellon Program of Morehouse College.

Former associates (and their descendants) of Lugenia Hope, members of the Morehouse College Alumni, professors, staff, and students of the Atlanta University Center have all encouraged my efforts on this project throughout the years. The Center has provided forums for dialogue, oral histories, artifacts, and much excitement. Members of the Inquirers, especially Mae Harvey and Vivian Beavers, reconstructed the overall heritages of the Inquirers and the Gate City Day Nursery Association. The Morehouse Alumni told me all I will ever need to know about "The House." For all the support from the total Atlanta University Center family, "much obliged."

To all my extended families, I owe you my strength. From the Wares of Macon, who allowed me space for solace; to the Harrises of Chicago, who fed, housed, and chauffeured me around Chicago; to the Denards of Atlanta, who walked, talked, read, reread, and nurtured this "child" with me, I am grateful. To my birth families—Rouses, Oakcrums, Thompsons—to those who announced loudly and proudly that "she's got her blue papers," to those who had talked Lugenia into print years before now, to all of those whose roots spring from the scenic hills and valleys of Nelson County, Virginia, I am who I am because of you.

Lastly, I extend appreciation to the editors of the University of Georgia Press and to special editor, Janis Bolster, for their assistance in this project.

Lugenia Burns Hope

Black Southern Reformer

Introduction

The Southern Network

In 1915 southern Black women attended the national meeting of the YWCA (Young Women's Christian Association) in Louisville, Kentucky, in an early step toward integrating the organization. Southern Black participation in the YWCA was then limited to Black collegiate branches. To rectify this systematic omission, Black delegates went to the Louisville meeting to learn how to extend the creation of Black branches into their own communities. Lugenia Burns Hope, already a seasoned reformer, was among this group of delegates. When the National Board of the YWCA eventually informed these Black women that they had endorsed the policy that gave southern white women control over the progression of Black branches, a vigorous controversy broke out. The campaign for Black autonomy in the organization was to be one of Hope's most heated battles in a career of community activism.

World War I interrupted this effort, but after the war Hope returned to Atlanta from Camp Upton on Long Island, New York, and picked up her struggles with the YWCA leadership. Her attempt to establish a Black branch in Atlanta, though supported and encouraged by local YWCA leaders, was opposed by the field supervisor for Colored Work in the South, headquartered in Richmond, Virginia. Hope had demonstrated that she could organize schoolgirls in Atlanta, yet she and her cohorts were informed that the decision to create a Black branch in Atlanta was not to be left to Black women, nor would Hope and her associates be allowed to choose a site for any Black branch that was permitted.[1]

Outraged, Hope's network of women became determined to put Blacks on an equal footing with whites in the YWCA. Demanding more sensitivity to local needs, they clarified for all concerned the principles on which work in their communities should be based. They insisted that Black delegates at the 1915 meeting had not approved of a policy that limited a Black branch's progress to the determination of the local white women. These educated, elite, middle-class Black women scoffed at the inference that they were incapable of choosing or serving as leaders. They decried the idea of southern white women directing Black community work. Hope challenged the competence of the field supervisor and charged her with excessive arrogance.[2] Hope and her associates petitioned to have southern colored work directed from national headquarters, to get Black representation on local committees and the National Board, and to acquire for Blacks the right of self-determination over their branches. Hope asserted that Black women should demand outright independent branches, responsible only to the National Board. She threatened that southern Black women would return to their churches and independent organizations before they consented to have southern white women, who knew absolutely nothing about them, controlling Black branches. Obstinate in its drive for self-determination, this group of southern Blacks continued for years to confront the Jim Crow policies of the YWCA.[3]

Lugenia Burns Hope began early on the career of community activism that would eventually distinguish her as a Black reformer. During her adolescent years in Chicago she worked with several charitable agencies, including Jane Addams's Hull House. She carried this involvement to Nashville, Tennessee, when as a new bride she accompanied her husband—leading Black intellectual and eventual college president John Hope—to Roger Williams University, where he was then an instructor. There she conducted classes in arts and crafts and in physical education for the female students. Within a year the Hopes moved again, this time to Atlanta. Soon after arriving, she became a member of the group of women who were working to provide day-care centers for the children of the West Fair community. This core group later became the founders of the Neighborhood Union, the first female social welfare agency for Blacks in Atlanta. For twenty-five years she led this agency in providing medical, recreational, educational, and civic services in Atlanta's Black communities. By 1930 the structure and policies of Hope's Neighborhood Union had been adopted by Haiti and Cape Verde in their efforts at community building.

During World War I, Hope, like other southern Black women as a group, responded wholeheartedly to the war effort. She and the Neighborhood Union conducted the YWCA's Atlanta War Work Council for Black soldiers. They petitioned for better police protection, access to public facilities, and the creation of more recreational centers. Hope's success at directing the Atlanta work led to her promotion to the position of national supervisor of the YWCA's Black hostess-house program, which provided recreational facilities for soldiers and centers for their families.

As a "race woman"[4] Hope worked to bring equality for all Americans through the NAACP (National Association for the Advancement of Colored People), the YWCA, the Urban League, and the Commission on Interracial Cooperation (later the Southern Regional Council); in conjunction with Jessie Daniel Ames, she also worked with the all-white Association of Southern Women for the Prevention of Lynching (ASWPL). She was, additionally, a member and/or official of the National Association of Colored Women's Clubs, the National Association of Colored Graduate

Nurses, the National Council of Negro Women, and the International Council of Women of the Darker Races.

As Hope rose on a national level because of her community, club, and settlement work, she was constantly in demand as a speaker. In 1927 she was a member of Herbert Hoover's Colored Commission, established to investigate the catastrophic flooding in Mississippi. Between 1920 and 1940 she served as an assistant to Mary McLeod Bethune in her capacity as director of the Negro Division of the National Youth Administration, helping to implement its programs in Black communities. Hope also lectured nationally for the National Council of Negro Women and served as an organizer of the National Association of Colored Graduate Nurses.

Southern Black women had a long history of organizing and implementing programs to improve the quality of life for Black southerners, especially Black women. Within their clubs, Black women instituted the services needed by their communities: daycare centers, kindergartens, medical clinics, reading rooms, libraries, settlement houses, mothers' meetings, literary clubs for young adults, academic and industrial arts classes, and homes for delinquent girls and boys. Southern affiliates of national organizations sought to provide these services in their own communities and, in addition, fought to establish in the South those facilities that were readily available to Black women in the North—such as Black branches of the YWCA. Members of these groups protested and petitioned against the law of "separate but equal," seeking the equality the nation professed. They struggled to get Black school facilities equal to those provided for whites, to have the standard of living in the Black communities equal to that in the white communities, and to obtain the hiring of Black personnel to service and to protect their communities. For example, city halls were bombarded with petitions initiated by these clubwomen demanding improvement in health services, police protection, and sanitation. Such voids in community services sparked the creation of neighborhood- and community-oriented clubs like Marion B. Wilkerson's Sunset Club of Orangeburg, South Carolina; the Tuskegee Woman's Club of Tuskegee, Alabama, founded by Margaret Murray Washington; the Woman's Industrial Club of Louisville, Kentucky, created by Nannie Helen Burroughs; Janie Porter Barrett's Locust Street Social Settlement of Peaks Turnout, Virginia; and, of course, the Neighborhood Union of Atlanta.

Hope belonged to the network of southern Black female activists who emerged regionally as the leaders and members of the clubwomen's national organizations, a group that included, in addition to those just named, Mary McLeod Bethune of Florida, Lucy Laney and Florence Hunt of Georgia, Nettie L. Napier and M. L. Crosthwait of Tennessee, Jennie Moton and Margaret Murray Washington of Alabama, Maggie Lena Walker of Virginia, and Charlotte Hawkins Brown and Mary Jackson McCrorey of North Carolina. These were women of impressive accomplishments. To take merely the example of Lucy Laney, founder of the Haines Normal and Industrial Institute: Laney, a member of the first graduating class of Atlanta University, began her teaching career in the public schools of Savannah. She was invited to Augusta, Georgia, by the Reverend William White, pastor of Harmony Baptist Church and one of the founders of Augusta Institute, later Morehouse College, who promised her the opportunity to open a school for Black youth. On January 6, 1886, Haines Institute opened with six students in the basement lecture room of a Presbyterian church.[5] Within two years, the school had grown enough to move into a new building. Laney's purpose was to train young people until they were thoroughly prepared to enter college courses without deficiences. Haines Institute progressed from an elementary school to a junior college, with a separate kindergarten and curriculum of manual and industrial classes also. Numbered among its distinguished alumni are Mary McLeod Bethune, Charlotte Hawkins Brown, Janie Porter

Barrett, and John, Thomas, Alethia, Jane, and James Birnie Hope. Jane Hope, later dean at Spelman College, was to praise Laney as "the most unselfish of the women who are engaged in public work. She has labored untiringly for the race, giving all and expecting nothing in return."[6]

A caucus of women of this caliber organized the Southeastern Federation of Colored Women's Clubs, which addressed in particular the plight of southern Black working women. By the beginning of the twentieth century, it was considered appropriate for employers to prefer white women over Black, because this preference matched the white public's perception of its own intellectual and moral superiority. As Sharon Harley has stated, the assumed inferiority of Black women translated economically into their higher concentration in low-paying, menial positions, their physical separation from white workers even at the same place of employment, and the large presence of married Black women in the labor force.[7] Southern Black women generally worked in either agriculture or domestic service.[8] The Southeastern Federation addressed the fact that Black domestics generally had to live in white households; that they had to work up to fourteen hours a day for extremely low wages; that they had only one afternoon off in two weeks to visit with their families; and that frequently they were the victims of sexual abuse, which forced them to choose between sexual submission to the man of the house and absolute poverty for themselves and their families.[9]

The Southeastern Federation also attacked the segregated facilities of the railroad system. A Black woman traveling by rail was forced to endure unpleasant racist encounters unless accompanying a white charge. In the latter case, the Jim Crow laws were temporarily revoked, a situation that produced more humiliation for the Black servant. A further target of the Southeastern Federation was the segregated school system of the South. This attack concentrated on the overcrowding of the classrooms; the double, maybe triple sessions; the low pay for the teachers; the dilapidated buildings; the poor ventilation; the lack of proper equipment and resources; and the high pupil-teacher ratio. Other focuses of attention from the southern network were the crop-lien system, the use of verbal contracts, and the convict-lease system. Clubwomen were especially appalled at the way Black women convicts were chained and stored with male convicts, at the sexual exploitation of these women by the white guards, and at the heavy tasks assigned to them regardless of gender or general health.

Members of the southern Black network saw themselves as role models—racial, moral, and female—for their less fortunate sisters. They believed that their mission of racial uplift had been inherited from foremothers like Sarah Remond, Maria Stewart, Harriet Tubman, Sojourner Truth, Frances Ellen Watkins Harper, and slave women who had a history of nurturing and bonding and what we now call networking.[10] These reformers saw their tradition and heritage as demanding commitment, responsibility, accountability, authority, self-respect, self-sufficiency, racial pride and solidarity, and a strong sense of noblesse oblige. They viewed their task as teaching—through the written text and the living example—refinement, culture, self-esteem, self-control, manners, morals, and high character in the Black community. In fact, many saw their organizations as the instruments for advancing the entire race.

Yet these reformers were not simply altruistic in their objectives. Educated Blacks of the early twentieth century were extremely concerned about the serious handicaps confronting them, handicaps that were not lessened by wealth or education. All southern Blacks were barred from hotels, restaurants, parks, and other public places. As Eugene Levy has noted, caste disabilities were color-blind. Middle-class Blacks argued that discrimination was in force because whites knew and associated with only the Black illiterate, ignorant, and criminal classes, who then became the representatives of the race. Members of the middle class believed that it was up to them to clean up this problem, to prove their mental and physical abilities and their readiness for equality.[11] Black women assumed the responsibility for proving their morality. They were ladies, they insisted, not gals or whores, a common nineteenth-century view. They argued that education would correct the race's weaknesses, while simultaneously raising the "ignorant above animal passion morality."[12] Moral improvement in the lower classes would generate both self-respect and respect from others. When whites became cognizant of the race's advancement, then caste would disappear.

Black women carried the virtues of Victorian America to the masses. They conducted clean-up campaigns to rid their communities of prostitutes, who, they charged, corrupted the younger girls. Margaret Murray Washington's Tuskegee Woman's Club brought the three B's—Bible, Broom, and Bath—to rural homes in Alabama, as Nannie Helen Burroughs's National Training School for Women and Girls taught them to young Black women in Washington, D.C. For it was the objective of the reformers to reform the masses, but even more, they wanted to expose to the better class of white America the better class of Black America. This emphasis on intraracial improvement, social, moral, and economic, reflected a general trend in Black thought during the early years of the century.

For the women of this southern network racial uplift was a priority; yet as Bell Hooks points out, Black women were no less committed to women's rights than white women were. Hooks maintains that nineteenth-century Black women were more conscious of their victimization by sexist oppression than any other female group in America society: "Their powerlessness was such that resistance on their part could rarely take the form of organized collective action. Because the white women's movement did not provide a forum for the grievances of Black women, Black women recognized the necessity to eliminate racism before they would have an equal voice in the women's movement." Segregated women's organizations were established for racial uplift and for the promotion of women's rights. Black women of the South understood the urgent need for the ballot. Suffrage, they believed, would mean the social equality of the sexes. As the ballot uplifted the race, it also would change the role of women in society, especially Black women as they aimed at solving specific problems uniquely theirs.[13]

Although several members of the southern network, among them Nannie Helen Burroughs, did not believe that Black women should take a passive position subordinate to men, and criticized those Black males who refused to support their efforts toward equal rights, in general these Black reformers differed from their white contemporaries in that they did not define feminism as a response to Black male exploitation. Black men were not held exclusively accountable for the sexual discrimination practiced against Black women by whites of both sexes. Several Black women's clubs, including the Neighborhood Union, allowed Black men to become auxiliary members. Also, many members of the southern network were married to "race men"—men like John Hope—who were vocal supporters of the network's racial and sexual consciousness.

Hope and her husband encouraged each other's work. Setting priorities was inevitable, however, and for Lugenia Burns Hope, as for other married women of the southern network, the roles of helpmate and mother were secondary to the commitment to social reform. Employed domestics and student assistants freed them from daily household responsibilities, thus making their public careers possible. Constant absences from home and family members did provoke feelings of guilt among these women, for Hope and her cohorts wholeheartedly supported the role of motherhood and believed in the nurturing characteristics of women as a group. They agreed with others of the Victorian era that a woman's instincts were more virtuous than a man's and that the woman was responsible for the moral character of the family. But Hope and this contingent of southern female reformers, many of whom were educators, college presidents or founders, wives of college presidents, and social workers, believed that they were ordained by an ancestral mission to carry their message of uplift—racial and feminine—to larger arenas.

Chapter One

A Spirit of Independence

Lugenia Burns Hope was born on February 19, 1871, to Ferdinand and Louisa M. Bertha Burns in St. Louis, Missouri. On both sides, however, her roots were deep in Mississippi.

Ferdinand Burns was a prosperous carpenter who had learned the trade as an apprentice to his father, William Burns. William Burns, the secretary of state of Mississippi during the 1850s, acquired a fortune in the manufacture of plows. By Rachel Burns he fathered five mulatto children: William, Jr., a blacksmith; Clay, a bricklayer; Sarah, a "lady of Natchez"; Randolph, a "gentleman without a trade"; and Ferdinand. Though such interracial marriages were illegal in antebellum America, the Burnses lived openly as a family in a colonial home at 500 Pine Street in Natchez, according to family records.[1]

Louisa Bertha was born in Natchez, but her family had immigrated to Mississippi from Canada before the Civil War. Her father is described in family records as a "retired capitalist of French descent." She was one of five children, the others being Samuel, Abraham, Delia, and Caroline. Like Ferdinand's, Louisa's family was mulatto, though the retired Frenchman had two white children, Louise and Joseph. Louise Bertha Ballard became a plantation mistress in Louisville, Kentucky, who raised horses and owned and operated a flour mill; her husband was appointed assistant secretary of labor by President Woodrow Wilson in 1913. Joseph Bertha served as the overseer on his sister's plantation. The family records refer to him as a "mean man"—mean enough so that when he was once shot by one of his sister's slaves, Louise took no action.[2]

When William Burns, Sr., died, several of his nephews from New Jersey came to Natchez to settle his estate. The nephews found Rachel's family, whom they attempted to sell into slavery. A white friend of Rachel's, Charles A. Lacoste, an accountant for a local bank, placed the family in protective custody until he could convince the white Burnses not to sell their Black relatives. Eventually Rachel and her children were released from jail and given their freedom. Lacoste then married Louisa Bertha's sister, Delia. Subsequently, they and their two sons moved to the township of Central, Missouri. Edward, the older son, became a detective with the Pinkerton Detective Agency and was involved with the apprehension of Jesse James. The second son, Henry, died young. When Lacoste died his widow inherited property valued at fifteen thousand dollars, although his will had to withstand a challenge raised by Lacoste's nephews from Baton Rouge, Louisiana. After the nephews' challenge failed, Delia sold the property and moved into the city of St. Louis, purchasing a house on Caroline Street. Her sister Louisa moved in with her to be near Ferdinand Burns, who had secured a carpenter's job in the city.

The exact date of the marriage of Ferdinand Burns and Louisa Bertha is not known. By 1880 they were residing in the central township of St. Louis with their seven children: William III, Redford, Ophelia Rachel, Charley Randolph, Joseph F., Adolph L., and Lugenia D.[3] Ferdinand's success as a carpenter allowed him to purchase a small farm and to prosper for a while. After his somewhat sudden death, the family moved further into the city, living on Seventeenth and then on Eighteenth Street. But his widow became very anxious that her position in the community would diminish. She decided to move to Chicago in order to start over and to provide Lugenia, the youngest, with better educational facilities than were available in St. Louis.

The Burnses relocated to Chicago during the pre-migration period of the late nineteenth century.[4] By 1870 Blacks numbered five thousand out of a citywide population of two hundred thousand. These Blacks were descendants of free persons of color: emancipated Blacks, those who had secured their freedom through self-purchase, and those who had secured it by fleeing the slaveholding states. Following emancipation, Chicago—formerly a station on the Underground Railroad—became saturated with segregationist thoughts and actions. Some white Chicagoans believed that the solution to the new Black migration and the older Black settlements was colonization. White laboring groups of foreign origins feared Black competition for their jobs and saw Blacks mainly as strikebreakers. Other white Chicagoans promoted the passage of Jim Crow laws and the implementation of discriminatory barriers. Yet Blacks were determined to remain a permanent part of even segregated Chicago. They established important institutional bases: churches, lodges, educational centers, social organizations. By 1885 their activism, with the assistance of a progressive political liberal faction, had ushered in the ballot, equality in law, and guarantees against discrimination in the use of public facilities.[5]

The Burnses entered Chicago along with many professional Blacks from the South. In this migration DuBois's "Talented Tenth" sought better economic, social, and political opportunities, yet they found shortages in housing and limitations in employment possibilities. They discovered that most Black Chicagoans were pigeonholed into semiskilled, unskilled, or menial positions. Nonetheless, the Black Belt (defined as such by 1893), where most Blacks were concentrated, had its own hospital; nurses' training school; branches of the YWCA, the National Negro Businessmen's

League, the NAACP, and the Federated Women's Clubs; and four newspapers.[6] The most prominent of the early newspapers was the *Conservator,* edited by Ferdinand Barnett, the husband of Ida Wells-Barnett. The *Conservator* announced that its mission was to be "a means of expression for Negroes and to aid in the promotion of the welfare of the Negro group." It would be, it promised, "devoted to the idea of stressing the importance of education, social uplift, and correct living."[7] Like civic and social groups, the Black papers called for racial pride and uplift, self-reliance, economic solidarity, patronage, and the development of strong and viable political alliances in the Black Belt.

Political activism was a tradition in Black Chicago, dating back to the antebellum era. By 1894 most Black Chicagoans were Republicans, though some were experimenting with the Democratic party. Black Chicagoans served on the county commission and in the state legislature. In 1894 Edward H. Wright was elected to the county commission and even succeeded in manipulating his election to its presidency. He managed the nomination and/or appointment of several other Blacks to political office, including the appointment of Ferdinand Barnett as the assistant state attorney.[8]

The Burns family quickly learned that its new city had class stratification within the Black community. Louisa, who had worried about her declining status in St. Louis, found that Black Chicago was divided into three class-conscious groups: first, the refined, those of education, breeding, and position, people like the Barnetts, the Williams—Fannie Barrier and S. Laing; next, the respectables, those who were poor but who were churchgoers, though too emotional in their worshiping; and finally, the riffraff or sinners, those who were unchurched and undisciplined.[9] The Black Old Settlers viewed the Great Migration of the early twentieth century with disdain, even though they would profit from this expanded consumer and electorate market. The Old Settlers saw nineteenth-century Chicago as a place of refinement, little prejudice, good race relations, and abundant employment. The nonprofessional southern migrants of 1915 and later would make it harder for all Blacks, for the increase in numbers would trigger racial conflicts, segregation, and discrimination. Thus the Burnses' move to Chicago during the pre-migration era was well timed: it meant that the young men of the family would find work and Lugenia would have educational opportunities beyond those offered in her native St. Louis. This move was also to bring her introduction to the community building and organizing that would become her life's work.

By the time Louisa moved to Chicago, her main responsibility was this youngest child, Lugenia, or "Genie." Ophelia, the older daughter, who had attended and taught school in St. Louis, married James Bryant on November 21, 1881 (Ida Wells-Barnett was one of the witnesses), and in the next few years gave birth to three daughters: Mellie (1883), Estella (1884), and Emma (1886). The Bryants then moved to Chicago, where Ophelia continued to teach and her husband became a successful businessman. By 1895 the Bryants had purchased a home at 6432 Champaign Street, which would become the home base for Lugenia after the death of her husband. Lugenia's brothers found jobs in Chicago also. Charley, who had worked as a laborer with a railroad company in St. Louis, in Chicago became a bookbinder with a Catholic publishing firm, following his conversion to Catholicism. Adolph was able to get a job at a bank, and Joseph found work in a millinery store. With these sources of support, Lugenia was able to go to school and her mother was free to remain at home.

Between 1890 and 1893, according to Lugenia's own records, she attended high school (the school's name is omitted), special study classes (probably with the girls of the Kings Daughters Association, where she worked as a secretary), the Chicago School of Design, the Chicago Business College, and the Chicago Art Institute. Available records for the latter do show her enrollment for the school year from October 1891 to June 1892. She began her studies in elementary classes, which worked in charcoal from antique fragments; she progressed into the intermediate classes, which worked with still life in monochrome and pen-and-ink; and she completed the year in the antique class, where she worked on models and designs.[10] Later she would draw on this training to offer sculpture classes to talented art students at Morehouse and Spelman colleges (working out of the attic of her home) and to teach arts and crafts to neighborhood children in the settlement house of the Neighborhood Union.

Lugenia's schooling ended rather abruptly. Charley got married, Adolph lost his job at the bank, the company where Joseph had been working went out of business. Lugenia gave up her school days to become the breadwinner for her household. For eight years she worked both as a bookkeeper for the Acme Printing and Engraving Company and also as a dressmaker. She left these jobs when she was appointed the first Black secretary to the Board of Directors of Kings Daughters, a charity organization that worked with the sick and needy, helped to bury the poor, and provided services to teenage working girls. Lugenia later described the work of the organization: "We decided to keep the club open until 8 o'clock to give the girls some place to stay while waiting for their trains to go home. So [we were giving] them the opportunity to study. We supplied an instructor for any subject that was desired by at least five girls. We got the instructors [from] the University of the City. I directed this work from 5–7 o'clock three nights per week."[11]

While working with Kings Daughters, Lugenia met the woman who was about to begin her directorship of the Silver Cross Club, an organization that operated cafeterias for businessmen and women in the Loop area of Chicago. Lugenia remembered:

> This woman [Mrs. Warne] came to my desk one afternoon and asked me to write my whole name in her book. After that she remarked—"I knew you were the woman I have been looking for. I am going to open a business and I want you to help me to make it a success." I did not want to leave the girls. She wanted me to be the manager of her new business operating from eight to twenty men and women, largely women, with the privilege of being at the club from five to seven o'clock three nights per week.[12]

Though reluctant to accept the attractive offer if it meant giving up her work with the Kings Daughters, Lugenia believed that she could handle both positions. She accepted and assumed the role of Warne's personal secretary, also assisting her at Hull House once a week, where Lugenia subsequently recalled meeting the great social worker Jane Addams.[13] She remained with both organizations and worked also as foreman for Warne Addressing Establishment until her marriage in 1897.

Lugenia later described the work of her Chicago years as a "rich and thrilling experience." The major attraction seems to have been that she could make a positive difference in people's lives: "I have always felt it the privilege of my life to have had that rich experience—their [club patrons'] joys and sorrows were poured into my ears and heart. They came for advice—as young as I was. We thought these problems through and they were helped."[14] Many years and community projects later, she credited her club work in Chicago with having given her the idea of community organization to prevent crime and poverty.

Lugenia's Chicago years taught her, in addition, that she could be happily self-sufficient. They left her with the expectation of working hard, thinking for herself, and meeting ambitious goals—experiences that gave her a lasting habit of independence.

This habit made her reluctant to accept false promises from prospective suitors, promises that did not allow her the same amount of autonomy. Being fiscally responsible for her family over a long period of time led her to be very wary about the men she dated. They had to assure her that they could afford to marry and begin a family while understanding that her house was her domain and that their moneys were her moneys also.

In 1893 the World's Columbian Exposition was held in Chicago in celebration of the four-hundredth anniversary of Christopher Columbus's landing in America. The United States invited the nations of the world to participate. This invitation, however, did not include Black Americans. Black representation at the fair was limited to the independent republic of Haiti, which erected a building on the fairgrounds and selected a former U.S. minister to Haiti, Frederick Douglass, to speak for the Haitian government. The exclusion of American Blacks became a subject of controversy. Douglass, Ida Wells-Barnett, and Frederick J. Loudin (of the Fisk Jubilee Singers) were able, through personal appeals to Black and women's groups of Chicago, to raise enough funds to publish a pamphlet, *The Reason Why the Colored American Is Not in the World's Columbian Exposition,* for circulation at the fair. Ten thousand copies of this "clear, plain statement of facts concerning the oppression put upon the colored people in the land of the free and home of the brave" were handed out during the fair's last three months.[15] Eventually the manager of the exposition, motivated by the popularity of the Haitian building and the widespread interest in Black issues expressed by visitors, responded to the protest against government-supported segregation by setting aside August 25, 1893, as Negro Day. Although this belated offer roused still more indignation, Douglass agreed to arrange the program, and the day ended with Paul Lawrence Dunbar, then a mere elevator boy from Dayton, Ohio, reading from his collection of poems, *Oak and Ivy.* Indeed, the event was a great success.

Festivities were held throughout the city in association with the exposition. The Columbian Dancing Party, sponsored by the Nogolese Club, took place on August 21, 1893. The evening was a gala event, with grand marches, waltzes, quadrilles, and polkas from the Second Regiment Band. Lugenia Burns attended, chaperoned by Chicago's prominent Black physician, A. M. Curtis, and his wife; and during the evening she met a Georgia-born theology student from Brown University, John Hope. On this occasion Lugenia, then an "undeniably pretty" young woman with "sun-rich coloring," did not find John Hope especially dashing, but she did find that the "steady gaze from his blue eyes made her quite uncomfortable."[16] John Hope invited her to the fair and she accepted. For the remainder of the summer the two dated on picnics and boat rides. Once the summer concluded, John returned to classes at Brown. Then he wrote Lugenia asking if she would help out a friend of his who might be coming to Chicago. She consented to do so but decided that John was using this request to extend their friendship. Gradually the two began to correspond. As the volume of the letter writing increased, John and Lugenia became more and more important to each other.

After graduating from Brown in 1894, John accepted a position as a classics instructor at Roger Williams University, a Black coeducational institution in Nashville, Tennessee. Over the next several summers he continued his course work at the University of Chicago, where he could be near Lugenia. By 1896 he had proposed to her several times and had become well acquainted with the heartaches and setbacks that marked their long courtship.

Chapter Two

For Love and Honor

Although by 1896 John had asked Lugenia to marry him on several occasions, Lugenia had avoided his proposals. In fact, she had not revealed their relationship to her family. Then in the summer of 1896 John wrote Lugenia that he had thus far respected her wishes but now believed that she was being too difficult. He had attempted, and she had acknowledged his efforts, to be generous to her moods, but now she was trying his "patience and heart to the utmost."[1] Lugenia understood his dilemma; still, she insisted, the time was not right to make their relationship public.

Lugenia was under extreme pressure from the numerous hats that she wore. For years she had been the main fiscal support of her mother's household. She worked two, sometimes three, jobs in order to care for herself, her mother, and any other unemployed family members who were temporarily or permanently living at their LaSalle Street address. These responsibilities brought her grave anxieties about leaving her mother, now aging and deaf, and about placing her personal happiness before her mother's welfare. The idea of abandoning her caused Lugenia to suffer severe guilt attacks, which contributed to a state of constant poor health. Louisa Burns played on her daughter's love by constantly pleading with her not to leave. Lugenia came to believe that if she did move away from her mother, some "dismal mishap" would befall the family.[2] She could not deny her need for John and her love for him, but she was not comfortable enough to approach the subject with her mother.

In the meantime, Lugenia's social life did not suffer. She was popular with several prominent gentlemen of wealth to whom she had been introduced through the Curtises, the Barnetts, and Ophelia and James. At one time she had four Chicagoans vying for her hand in marriage. Her family encouraged her to select from this group, for marriage would mean that she would still live in Chicago and she would be marrying into economic security. Lugenia wrote John about her prosperous gentlemen friends and wanted to know how he fared economically in relation to them. She wondered if she would be as comfortable with him as with any of his competition.

The family disapproval of John was mainly influenced by Louisa's feelings. John was too poor, as Louisa saw it; he was only a struggling college teacher in a small Black college in Tennessee, and he would carry her daughter away from her to the rabidly racist climate of the South. Mostly, however, her disapproval stemmed from John's failure of etiquette in not having asked her for her daughter's hand in marriage. To Lugenia's brothers, John was "an annoyance." They too desired their baby sister to choose from among her Chicago suitors and remain in the Windy City. Still, Lugenia could not stop writing to and caring about her "Jack." Insecure about his motivations, she accused him frequently of thinking less of her, even though his letters were lengthy declarations of his love and desire for her. Her clandestine letters were passionate ones, showing how she envisioned their life together. Yet Lugenia was not ready to give up the chase. She enjoyed John's frequent proposals and the constant attention she received from the men in Chicago. She was indeed in charge of her love life. This independent twenty-five-year-old did not change her mind about John until he assured her that he had "withdrawn himself from other women and now was exclusively hers."[3] This step marked a change in their relationship.

In September Lugenia finally said yes to John. The two then became very open with their affection toward each other. While John was on a visit to Chicago, Joseph witnessed them kissing. John wrote Lugenia, who was uneasy about the incident, that he was glad it had happened, for now her family would "understand that we love each other and that there is nothing secretive about our feelings." Louisa was furious at her daughter and John. Not only was their behavior inappropriate, she insisted, but the two were making fools of themselves. She wanted the relationship to end and Lugenia to remain in Chicago. John was convinced that he could change his soon-to-be mother-in-law's mind by explaining how much he loved her daughter. Meanwhile, he was afraid that Lugenia would succumb to her mother's dictates. He wrote Lugenia that he hoped that her mother would not like him any less now that she knew he loved her daughter. "Still I cannot promise her I shall love you less even to win her esteem. Tell her I love you as your father loved her and with God's help I shall never love you less." John assured his Genie that he was an honorable person and he desired her family to know this. He told her that he could endure their unanimous contempt "if I still have your love."[4]

In October Lugenia received her diamond ring, an heirloom of John's father's. John admitted to her that he knew it was small, but at least it would tell her family that he was in earnest. If it was not large enough, then he would purchase what she liked. Lugenia responded that the ring was extremely "little," but she did not return it.[5]

Lugenia, now officially engaged, extracted several promises from her fiancé before the nuptials. She believed that her marriage would work only with mutual respect. She demanded that her household be hers alone. Once pressed, John assured her that she would be the "queen" and he the king. "We are to control our little realm 'mutually'[;] neither of us is to be the servant, yet both of us gladly serve each other in love and patience." Lugenia remained concerned that the Hopes, who approved of her, would interfere. This fear took on substance for Lugenia after she learned that they were furnishing the home in Nashville she would share with John. Lugenia, beside herself with anger, reminded John that she had given up men with money for him, believing that he was a real man. Was he after all too poor to marry? John begged her not to dwell constantly on his economic status. They both knew he had little. He was not, he assured her, controlled by his family. "I tell my people none of our business as a rule. You know everything I have told them, for I have told you what I told them." Yet Lugenia was not certain that she would come first with him, and she knew from personal experience the unhappiness this could cause. She demanded that he examine the possibility that he might have to make a choice between her and his family. He had always told his people, he replied, that they would not have any influence on his choice of a mate, adding, "I feel that those life questions ought to be handled by the two who are to profit or suffer by their solution."[6]

John intended for their marriage to liberate Lugenia from her jobs and her fiscal responsibility to her family. He saw her service with the various social work agencies in Chicago, an approved nineteenth-century female occupation, as work and not a career. He did not appear to understand that this reform work was very important to Lugenia and that she saw these experiences as the foundation of a lifetime of community building and organizing. Thus when Lugenia asked what she would be doing in Nashville, John dismissed the question by telling her that she could perform some of her social work on Nashville's "little green girls." He intended her to be his wife, a career in itself, and to concentrate on supporting and nurturing his needs and desires. He did not want her to worry about Nashville or about their future. In fact, one of his colleagues had asked about possibly moving to Atlanta. He solicited Lugenia's opinion. When she responded in favor of the idea, he wrote her that he was glad that she was interested in "his" affairs, for "that is what you are born for: so that, in assisting me, you are simply doing that which you were born to do."[7] John would soon learn that Lugenia's spirit of independence did not mysteriously disappear now that she was to become Mrs. John Hope.

By December Lugenia was having second thoughts. She now decided that her life's role should be as a missionary in Africa. Earlier she had persuaded John not to pursue a career in the ministry. Using a similar argument, John convinced her that their feelings were sincere and that they were worthy of happiness. With the assistance of Ophelia and Charley, the other Burnses finally blessed the marriage. Louisa was still convinced that her daughter would incur some horrible fate in going south, but she too accepted John. Thus 1897 brought support and encouragement to Lugenia and John from both families as they prepared for a Christmas wedding. By September final plans were made. On December 29, 1897, one day after filing for their marriage license, Lugenia and John were married by the Reverend Moses H. Jackson, pastor of Lugenia's church, Grace Presbyterian. She was twenty-six, he was twenty-nine. Having been given Charley's pledge to care for their mother, Lugenia left with her husband for Tennessee.

When the Hopes reached Nashville at the beginning of the winter semester, they were met at the station by J. W. Johnson, a colleague and friend of John's. Arriving on campus at one in the morning did not, to John's surprise, deter the celebration that had been planned for them. They found

> the doorway to the boys' building, where the Hopes were to live, ablaze and a carpet laid for the entrance of the bride and groom. Inside, the staircase was lined with boys holding lamps. And there

was . . . a banquet and cordial speeches of welcome. These were still the days when John was disposed to be silent and rather shy. But his bride was neither and the wedding party went off with gayety. The sense that everybody liked him and was glad to welcome him—the friendship and goodwill—had never before been so articulate, so dramatically displayed. It was good that he could bring Genie to a place where she could feel that he was firmly established.[8]

Lugenia entered into the spirit of the place, developing friendships with female students at Roger Williams and starting a class in physical education. Simultaneously she was introduced to the "colored" society of Nashville, as she and her husband became frequent guests of the Honorable James Napier, registrar of the Treasury of the United States from 1909 to 1912, and his wife, Nettie. These contacts also brought entree to the local "colored" literary and debating clubs and societies.

The settling-down period had barely begun when uncertainty crept in. From the moment John had left Brown University, moving to Nashville had fulfilled part of his desire to return south, but he had always envisioned returning to his "dearly loved home of Georgia."[9] The place he most desired to teach was Atlanta Baptist College, but since his graduation there had been no openings on the faculty. In April 1898, however, the president of the school, George Sale, invited John to come to Atlanta to teach classics. A week or so later he offered John an extra job as bookkeeper, which would bring his proposed salary to eight hundred dollars. Though desperately wanting to relocate to Atlanta, John pondered the offer for a month, finally deciding in late May to accept the invitation. His appointment was to begin in the fall of 1898, so barely six months after establishing residence in the city of Nashville, the new bride was preparing to move further into the Deep South.

The Hopes spent the summer in Chicago, where a Society of New York scholarship allowed John to undertake further study at the University of Chicago. The summer months gave Lugenia some time to spend with her family, especially her mother, before the relocation to Atlanta.

The Hopes moved to Atlanta in the fall of 1898, taking up residence in Graves Hall. Atlanta Baptist College had been founded in Augusta in 1867 as Augusta Institute, with the goal of educating the new freedmen. From classes that began in the basement of Springfield Baptist Church, the school moved to the basement of Atlanta's Friendship Baptist Church in 1879 and became Atlanta Baptist Seminary. A building was erected at Elliot and Hunter streets, near the Southern Railroad Terminal, and classes were conducted there in competition with the loud noises of rumbling trains. The school then purchased fourteen acres of its current site, on West Fair and Ashby streets. In 1897 the Superior Court of Fulton County granted it a charter to become a college and the school was renamed Atlanta Baptist College, becoming a permanent part of the West Fair community. In 1913 it was renamed in honor of Henry L. Morehouse, a major benefactor, supporter, and trustee of the college, and hence became Morehouse College.[10] The main building, Graves Hall, included dormitory rooms, classrooms, a dining hall, and the president's office. A second building, Quarles Hall, was soon put up to relieve the classroom and office-space crisis.

John was hired as an instructor of classics, both Greek and Latin. His students found him challenging but also a friend and mentor, one they sought out for guidance. Because of its growing popularity, John introduced football to the college in 1898–99 as the beginning of an athletic program for the school. He also became one of President Sale's advisers and confidants.

Atlanta Baptist College's curriculum in 1898 was in four divisions: the English Preparatory Department, providing elementary development; the Academic Course, which offered high school work (there were no Black high schools in the state or in the South prior to 1924); the College Course; and the Divinity School. The student body numbered 146 and the faculty included people like Waldo B. Truesdell, Carrie Bemus, John Hubert, and William E. Holmes. Holmes, who was popular with the students, had served the college for twenty years under four presidents as professor of history and English, secretary of the faculty, and librarian. In 1898 he became pivotal in a crisis that had been brewing on the campus for some time, a crisis that caught John in the middle. Black Georgia Baptists, one of the groups who had founded the college (along with the American Home Mission Society of the North), had gradually become disillusioned with the white leadership of Black education in the South, including the tenure of George Sale as president of Atlanta Baptist. While acknowledging the vital role of whites after the Civil War, the Blacks had decided that they were ready to assume command of their children's education. The northern whites disagreed and charged them with being ungrateful to their white friends and benefactors. Moving ahead in spite of this opposition, the Black Baptists chose Holmes to engineer the ouster of Sale from Atlanta Baptist College. The attempt failed. Holmes then left the college and moved to Macon, where he opened Central City College in the expectation that much of the Atlanta Baptist student body would follow him. His hope was dashed: the students elected to stay at their former location.[11] John, although he was Holmes's friend, also stayed on at Atlanta Baptist, acting as Sale's main assistant and being groomed to succeed him as president.

Atlanta Baptist College was surrounded by the campuses of Spelman College, Atlanta University, and later Morris Brown and Clark colleges. Faculties of Spelman and Atlanta Baptist Colleges shared classrooms and taught some classes at each institution. Faculties from all of the schools worked together on projects promoting racial consciousness. One of the Hopes' new friends in Atlanta was W. E. B. Du Bois, a professor of economics and history who had arrived at Atlanta University in 1897, brought in to direct the Atlanta Conference on Negro Problems that the university was inaugurating. John Hope and Du Bois eventually emerged not only as educators but as race men of the early twentieth century, firm advocates of equal justice for Black Americans. By definition this stance made them opponents of Booker T. Washington's accommodationist theories on education, political, and civil rights for Blacks. The two men were also a part of an early plan, never realized, to build an all-Black colony in south Georgia.

Du Bois, who knew of Lugenia's social reform work in Chicago, invited her to attend an upcoming conference (held in 1899 or 1900) on the topic "The Welfare of the Negro Child." This conference was planned by Gertrude Ware, the kindergarten-training school teacher at Atlanta University and sister of the president. She led a discussion on the care of children whose mothers had to work and who were therefore left daily either in locked homes or wandering unattended in the city streets. Some of the mothers at the meeting decided to try to establish free kindergartens so that mothers who had to work could have facilities at which to leave their preschoolers for at least half of each school day. Following the conference Ola Perry, who had trained under Ware, began the first school in her home. Ware met with Ida Wynn and Mrs. Brynard Burch in Wynn's home and decided to ask several women to help them finance the effort. A board was established, consisting of Adrienne Herndon, Mary Gaines, Betty Jones, Nettie Towns, Ruth Carey, Mrs. Donerell Green, William G. Alexander, D. Anderson, David T. Howard, Burch, Wynn, and Lugenia Hope. They called the group the Gate City Free Kindergarten Association. Lugenia accepted the chairmanship of a committee to raise money, noting:

> When Commencement was over I was Chairman of a Committee of twenty women whose duty it was to raise money to open one kindergarten in the fall except two . . . women were not interested.

The two felt that it was no use, we could not do it alone but I told them if they would stand-by we would offer the opportunity for the under-privileged children in the fall. We got a new committee that would work and opened two kindergartens that fall and two more the next year.[12]

Among the people asked to contribute was Alonzo Herndon, founder of the Atlanta Life Insurance Company. He was sufficiently impressed with the association's goals and accomplishments so that he purchased a large old stone building in White's Alley and gave it to the association to be used as a school and playground for the children. For several years he also paid for a teacher and daily milk delivery. With more room the kindergarten was enlarged to become a day-care center, as most of the children's parents worked all day. Soon four more kindergartens were opened throughout the city. Annual Thanksgiving dinners were sold to solicit money.

Lugenia had begun to be concerned about the children of the West Fair area almost immediately after her arrival. During her first night in Graves Hall she heard fighting, brawling, and pistol shots from outside the campus. Atlanta Baptist College was enclosed in a slum area, surrounded by sections like Beaver Slide and streets like Peters, Roach, Fair, Beckwith, Battle's Alley, and Low's Alley. These roads were unpaved, full of holes and debris (some of it dumped by the city), and without water mains; they stank and smoked. Activities in these areas terrified the neighborhood children.[13] Lugenia selected Battle's Alley as her project, deciding to try to reach the women on that street and to give special attention to their needs. Lugenia found that these working mothers needed full day-care centers and safe recreational lots where their children could play. She carried this information back to her kindergarten committee and tried to impress upon it that kindergartens could be transformed into community centers and that the kindergartens could be but one of many services rendered by the centers. She suggested that four such centers over the entire city of Atlanta be opened and that the work be expanded to include all areas of the city. The committee did not adopt her suggestion. The kindergarten association continued merely to operate day nurseries, now under the name the Gate City Day Nursery Association.[14]

The lack of recreational facilities for Black children in Atlanta was one of the reasons Herndon had purchased the building and land for the White's Alley kindergarten. Though Lugenia knew about this lack from her conversations with the mothers of Battle's Alley, it became clearer to her after the birth of her first son. Edward Swain Hope was born on August 28, 1901, in the small apartment on the second floor of Graves Hall (now Room 204). Because of John's horror of debt, the couple decided that buying a house was too hazardous; instead, they moved into a larger apartment on the first floor of Graves Hall. As Lugenia planned recreational activities for her child over the next few years, she discovered that facilities were nonexistent. The city of Atlanta did not provide a single playground or park for Black children. Angered, Lugenia rallied faculty wives and other women, many of them mothers, who lived in the neighborhood of Spelman and Atlanta Baptist colleges, urging them to meet in order to find some means of relieving the urgent need for play space for their children. The women were able to persuade the administration of Atlanta Baptist College to allow them to use part of the school's grounds for a playground. They supervised the children and hosted fund-raisers to purchase needed equipment. Local businesses were asked to donate some of the equipment and to provide the workmen to install it. Later this same nucleus of women began to inspect the community for other problems needing attention, laying the foundation for what would eventually become well-known community organizations like the Neighborhood Union, the Atlanta branch of the Southeastern Federation of Colored Women's Clubs, and the Women's Committee for the Improvement in the Colored Public Schools.[15] Lugenia's community reform work always centered on improving living conditions and future opportunities for children. This protectiveness arose out of her desire to provide the best possible environment for her own sons. Her second son, John II, was born on Christmas Day in 1909. The family had moved from the cramped dormitory quarters to the president's house in 1906, following John's inauguration as Atlanta Baptist College's first Black president.[16] As John II subsequently described this home, the first and second floors included a living room; a dining room; front, back, and second-floor porches; a kitchen; a foyer; a room behind the kitchen; two staircases; bathrooms; and four bedrooms. The third floor served periodically as lodging for female student workers, single white female teachers, and Lugenia's niece, Emma, a student at Spelman; it also provided a classroom for Lugenia's sculpture classes and a closet that she used as a darkroom for her photography.[17]

As homebuilder, Lugenia sought to create order and discipline while she instilled constructive ideas and objectives into her children—and generally saw them carried out. Discipline in the Hope house was based on agreement and respect, sometimes teasing, but rarely fear. John II remembered later that his Saturday chore was to clean thoroughly the big white bathroom tub on the second floor. Each Saturday morning he tried to stall the inevitable as long as possible. After several calls, his mother would come into his room, call his name, reach under the bedcovers, and wiggle his big toe, saying, "John, oh John, wake up and look at your beautiful mother."[18] This was generally impetus enough for him to get up and get busy. He recalled that his mother had an uncanny ability to use the lecture as an effective means of discipline. She calmly talked to her boys about whatever they had done, going over their misdeeds and expressing her disappointment in them. She also relied on neighbors and other adults to oversee her children. Any reports of misbehavior were dealt with promptly, and she used physical punishment when she thought it was warranted.

Though both Hopes traveled extensively, owing to their careers, and though both worried at times about these separations from the children, their sons reported as adults that they had not felt neglected. As John II recollected, both parents tried not to be away simultaneously. Moreover, when both were home their mother made an effort to bring the entire family together for meals and regular activities. John II got additional attention outside the family: because he was the youngest, the students adopted him as the mascot of the college, and several of them were assigned to watch over him. He was spoiled by constant notice and food, to the point where his mother made him wear a sign reading, "Please do not feed this animal."[19]

The Hope children were expected to be contributing members of the household. Edward provided one illustrative anecdote. Lugenia, the former dressmaker, made practically the entire wardrobe for herself and the younger members of the family, even such things as coats and suits for the boys. Edward recalled: "At the time there were few children in the area and I accompanied Mother to her class at Spelman. [She taught a millinery class there.] I too made articles and accessories; and at home I often worked the connecting rod on her foot-operated sewing machine, thus contributing my effort to the family output."[20]

Probably the clearest view of Lugenia, the mother, can be gained from a speech she gave under the title "Family Life as a Determinant in Racial Attitudes of Children." From it one can appreciate the task Black mothers faced in teaching their children about racism. She used one of her boys as an example. She had tried, she said, to teach both sons to respect women regardless of their race or station in life. One day she and one of her sons were coming home on a crowded streetcar. A white woman got on, and since there were no seats, her "little" son immediately got up and offered his, beside his mother. This caused a stir if not a racial "incident":

> If she had simply ignored the seat there would not have been any question but she made some demonstration which the child did not understand. This raised problems in his mind . . . , in spite of my effort to keep the truth from him. I did not want to burden his young life because I knew it would have to come all too soon anyway. The Negro mother has to pray for patience and insight lest she forget that above all her little ones must not become embittered. To make the little ones go to sleep or stop crying the Negro mother will hug the little child close and say "The Old White Man will get you if you don't stop crying." This brings results.[21]

Although life in the president's house was a refreshing change from Graves Hall, and one that gave the family more privacy, this could be interrupted by students or guests at any time: a Black college president "could never call his home his own," especially considering that black travelers faced discrimination and segregation in public accommodations. Edward called their home a sort of "defacto glorified guest house." His mother, he added, was the "heart, backbone, and prime mover in this large, but homey, guest house with its changing flow of transients from the poor unfortunates to the most successful and prominent, not only Negroes unable to stay in the hotels . . . but many whites and foreign visitors who preferred the campus to the city hotel." These included not only Black college teachers, presidents, and trustees but also distinguished guests like the headmaster from Worcester Academy, the president of Brown University, and various artists in different fields. Whether these guests stayed overnight or only for a meal, it was Lugenia who assumed the responsibility of seeing to it that things went smoothly and that her guests were happy—"no small job considering the tight budget and the necessarily continuous turnover of her student work force."[22]

One guest who spent several weeks with the Hopes was Madame Hackney, who trained the entire Atlanta Baptist College student body as a choir and then conducted this choir, accompanied by the school's small orchestra, in a full program of classical music—"Hiawatha's Wedding Feast," the "Hallelujah Chorus" from *Messiah,* and Negro spirituals ("to satisfy the white segregated audiences")—before a huge audience at the Armory Auditorium. This program "brought directly and indirectly a substantial amount of money and prestige to the college."[23]

Lugenia ran this "guest house" with assistance from family members, hired help, and student workers. Students from Spelman and Atlanta Baptist colleges were assigned to work in the president's house. One male student arrived at 5:45 each morning, awakening the family. Interestingly, his duties included dusting and sweeping the house. Another male, a nephew of John's named John Birnie, for a time was responsible for making the bread. All of the young, including the Hope sons, were assigned dishwashing. Periodically John Sr. contributed to the kitchen detail, but his efforts were sporadic. Lugenia organized and supervised the available workers into an effective force so that she had time for other duties—getting her children to Sunday School, for instance, and planning athletic events and family social activities, in addition to her responsibilities outside the home.

She also continued to care about the arts, adorning her walls with pictures (copies of classical works, scenes from history, and portraits of Black and Native American heroes), teaching sculpture, and getting interested enough in photography to develop and print her own negatives. She encouraged professional photographers like the popular Robert Scurlock, Sr., to tour the South and to record important figures in Black higher education. When the Inquirers, one of Atlanta's oldest social and literary clubs, formed in February 1909, Lugenia became one of the charter members. These original members were twelve of the women who had organized the Gate City Free Kindergarten Association. During a social gathering at the home of Ida Wynn, the twelve decided to establish a club to consider current events, to read and discuss Shakespeare, and to provide a means to fellowship. The club met monthly on Wednesday afternoons, a practice that is still continued.[24]

From the beginning John may have assumed that his new bride would be responsible primarily to him, now that he had liberated her from family and financial obligations. Lugenia was indeed supportive of her husband's work and on many occasions influenced his actions. Though not a participant in the day-to-day administration of either Atlanta Baptist College or Atlanta University (John became the university's first Black president in 1929 and served in that office until his death in 1936), she nevertheless encouraged John's ideas and efforts to raise funds for the schools' endowments and to secure influential contacts for the colleges. In a 1929 letter to her, John expounded on what a central force she was behind him:

> I wonder how it would have been if I had never met you. I am absolutely sure that I should never have had the success that I have had or risen to positions that have come to me. I bow down to you, my dear little wife, in reverence and love for what you are to me. I want you to know, too that I am not changed or puffed . . . about anything that has come to me. I want you to share it all with me—the honor and the money.[25]

On a trip aboard the *Maine,* he wrote his wife about his reluctance to make the trip and how she had persuaded him to go, adding that his hesitation had stemmed from his enjoyment of her and of being at home. Her influence on him was strong: "It seems that we have taken a new grip on each other and I am expecting a delightful year inspite of all problems. If you will just convince me that you believe I can swing the A.U. job I shall be almost perfectly happy. If you will first let me not feel that you are pushing me. But my dear, you are intense."[26]

On an earlier occasion, Lugenia had encouraged John to take a necessary trip that had in the end proved advantageous to the college. He credited her love, sacrifice, and urging: "If you had not urged me I do not think I should have come. I hope God will let me do some great big thing for you some day."[27]

From the very outset of their marriage, it was apparent that Lugenia's interest in reform had not abated. The move to Nashville gave her a small chance to continue her social work, and the move to Atlanta offered her an opportunity to be more active: within weeks of her arrival, she became affiliated with the Gate City Day Nursery Association. In time, and with the success of the Neighborhood Union's programs, Lugenia's involvement with community organization and its effective implementation became more time-consuming. Her expertise was in demand, and thus she began to travel extensively. Her reputation as a social worker grew and brought with it a new and expanded identity. Her affiliations increased, taking her more frequently away from her husband. His response was not always wholly supportive. Prior to ending a European tour, he wrote Lugenia:

> My stay is reaching its close. Eight days more and I shall be on the sea coming home[,] coming to you. How I dream of you all day long as I move about from place to place! Yet when I return you will be so busy that you will have no time to listen to me. Your work as mine takes me from you. You blame me, yet you are too busy for small talk. However, we have been a long time apart and "you" must be more with me.[28]

For Love and Honor

One might ask whether John became jealous of the time and energies that his wife was giving outside their home. Though Lugenia was a social worker, an acceptable female occupation, John still believed that the work was taking his wife away from him and his sons. Once Lugenia wrote him about a tennis game she and Edward had played. John, mildly interested in the game, emphasized to her how glad he was that she was spending time with Edward, adding his fear that the two of them had neglected the "little fellow" and had given him their tired and "fagged ends." He "charged" *her,* from his European location, to get to know Edward's cares and feelings.[29]

The fact remains that pressures and obligations did call for Lugenia to be on the move most of the time, but one wonders if she needed to be constantly on the move. We can only speculate about how their lengthy absences affected their marriage. Did Lugenia perhaps need new challenges and tasks in order to avoid feelings of loneliness and stagnation? John's letters to her while she was away suggest that her constant activity resulted from her inability to relax and enjoy past accomplishments. He told her that he could excel her in getting new joys out of old experiences. "I do not have to be doing things all the time. The things that have already been done have such a significance to me that they are life for me quite as much as the things I do anew." He warned her not to overextend herself and thus lose her "poise and self-control," for after all "doing things is not all of life." Instead, he hoped that she would drop her "feverishness," be content, and "store up a peace for the quiet years ahead."[30]

Fundamentally, John seems to have understood that her involvement with social welfare work in Atlanta was a natural carry-over from her Chicago days and was a major part of her character. On more than one occasion he commented on how caring a person she was, not only toward her family but toward others; that, he recognized, was what made her so special. For example, in a 1912 letter written aboard the *Lusitania* he observed: "You do things so naturally, you love and sacrifice so 'easily' that you are unusual. I believe it must be that quality in you which makes the Neighborhood Union people believe in you. They have got a glimpse of your real self and your real worth."[31]

This real self was a complex one. Edward Hope described his mother as "a fighter, usually happy, even gay, but with great determination. . . . She was not rash or insolent, rather . . . she was appraising and an organizer . . . quietly planning the step-by-step progress of each campaign."[32] Her cheerful determination could make room for playfulness—certainly this aspect is evident in the memories of her son John. Even late in her life she kept a fun-loving side. John II's wife, Elise, told this story of an outing with "Mother" Hope that took place in about 1945:

> One afternoon Elise, Linda, Jack, and Richard [John and Elise's children] and Mother Hope were outside in the back at a frog pond. . . . They had rolled up their pants, pulled up their dresses, hunting for tadpoles in the pond in the back, when little Linda said, "This would be a good time to go up to Bam-Mamma's" [this was Linda's name for her other grandmother, Cynthia Oliver, who lived in Kentucky]. Everyone agreed, and Elise asked Mother Hope, who grinned and agreed to go. Enthusiastically all five, along with the dog, plunged into the car, with only toothbrushes in hand, no sandwiches, no food, and began to drive 150–180 miles to Louisville, Kentucky, to Bam-Mamma's house. On the way, they were starving, so Elise stopped and Mother Hope bought a watermelon, which they cut and dived into, Mrs. Hope enjoying it also after taking her nitroglycerin pill. They arrived at Bam-Mamma's around dark. Elise rang the doorbell, and when her mother came and saw her and the children, not aware of Mrs. Hope's presence, she laughed at the idea that Elise and the children had just showed up on the doorstep. Then Mrs. Hope appeared. She attempted to climb the long stairs, laughing, taking four steps at a time, resting, and laughing heartily. After a long ordeal, four steps and resting, Mother Hope finally

completed the long steps to the top apartment. Mother Cynthia had a feast, cooking as if she was expecting them: hot rolls, turkey, macaroni and cheese, a feast! Then the two grandmothers retired out on the porch and sat in the two large chairs. When bedtime came, the boys were put in one area, Elise and Mother Cynthia and Linda slept on the porch, and Mother Hope was given the bedroom, near the closed porch to ensure comfort and silence. The next morning, with three children up and about, there was noise. But no noise came from the bedroom. Elise almost panicked, remembering that if anything happened to John's mother—for she had brought her to Louisville—he would never forgive her. She decided to look in on Mother Hope. There was a long form in the bed but no movement. Elise told her mother and both decided to wait a little longer before going into the room. Finally, out of fear and near panic, the two mustered up enough courage to enter the room, approaching the bed slowly. After standing by the bed in total fear they noticed that the bed was rocking. Mrs. Hope turned over, rolling in laughter, for she had been playing possum with them for the entire time. Elise and Cynthia, relieved yet overwhelmed, fell out in laughter.[33]

Lugenia's ability to juggle her roles as wife, mother, and activist came ultimately from her strength of character and the organization and structure she was able to bring to her days. Aiding her also were hired workers in her home, who freed her from many daily household chores. Yet what becomes vivid in examining Lugenia the homebuilder, the mother, and the wife is the control she exerted over most aspects of her life. Though committed to her husband and sons and the duties incurred in caring for them, she did not allow them to dominate her existence or her time. Her "take-charge" style and willingness to delegate tasks—characteristics of any good administrator—carried over into her domestic life. Probably these attitudes became instrumental in instilling in her children a certain spirit of independence. She commanded respect, gave love and encouragement, and in return was loved and respected by her family.

Lugenia supported her husband's careers, as professor and

president of Atlanta Baptist College and later Atlanta University, but her strong desire to work for reform in the Black community and the urgent need for that reform often took precedence over domestic concerns. Although these commitments frequently separated her from John and the children, still their support and understanding seem to have been profound.

Chapter Three

The New First Lady

In 1906 Atlanta was the scene of the South's most sensational race riot.[1] For months the city had been whipped into a fury of race hatred by efforts to disfranchise Blacks and by irresponsible journalism.

For over a year the leading gubernatorial candidates, Hoke Smith and Clark Howell, had centered their campaigns on the disfranchisement of Blacks. Smith, a cabinet member under former president Grover Cleveland, conducted a rabidly anti-Black campaign that had the support of white supremacist and ex-Populist Tom Watson. Denouncing Blacks as inferior beings and guaranteeing that suffrage would be completely denied them were he elected, Smith made inflammatory statements like "We will control the Negro peacefully if we can, but with guns if we must." He advocated enacting a constitutional amendment to control Black voting, as other southern states had done, for such an action would free elections of the "corrupt, ignorant vote of the Negro, but not deny suffrage to the illiterate whites."[2]

Clark Howell, editor of the Atlanta *Constitution,* condemned Smith's campaign as an attempt to use racism to support his own cause. He pointed out that the Fifteenth Amendment made disfranchisement unconstitutional and that in fact the party primaries, begun in 1877, had accomplished a de facto disfranchisement anyway. Smith nonetheless won an overwhelming victory.[3]

The radical and racial nature of the gubernatorial campaign continued to be a catalyst that sold newspapers even after the political contest was over. A survival struggle ensued, in which each of the evening papers, the Atlanta *Georgian*, the Atlanta *Journal*, and the Atlanta *News*, tried to outdo the others by exploiting sensational news and publishing numerous extras.

Extreme measures were instituted to attract readers. The best strategy for results proved to be the abuse of Blacks. John Temple Graves, in particular, reported Black violence in vivid detail in the *News*. Walter White, a native Atlantan, recalled later that such stories were standard and familiar and frequently ran as "eight column streamers instead of the two or four column ones."[4] Front-page headlines like "Insulting Negro Badly Beaten at Terminal Station," "Bold Negro Kisses Girl's Hand," "Empty Gun Saves Her," "Negro Grabs Girl as She Steps Out on Back Porch" appeared daily. Emphatic calls and pleas were made to southern white men to "protect" their women: "To think of the awful crimes being committed against our women is alarming. It seems that men are justified in adopting the most radical punishment for the perpetrations of such deeds that can be devised this side of the region of fire and brimstone. Then to Arms! Men of Georgia."[5] Sensational pieces of this sort were common, and unproved charges of assault upon white women by Black men were enough to incite mobs, giving them license to attack and in some cases murder innocent and unsuspecting Blacks.[6]

Such was the situation on Saturday, September 22. In rough notes written years later, Lugenia recalled the tensions in the city and the events surrounding the riot:

> Negroes [were] leaving the country and small towns for northern cities to escape [the] terrorizing effect of the campaign of hate.
>
> Negroes [were] not able to buy fire arms for months before the Riot.

Negroes were quite unsuspecting that their white friends had planned to destroy them. The Negro[es] will never forget or forgive the shock of realizing that their white friends had betrayed them. They should have protected their servants at least. When the storm broke it was Sat. night when Negroes were doing their marketing for Sun. They were at the market with their whole family. Out of a clear sky the white people began kicking—beating. They would stop the street cars, pull the Negroes out to beat them—Some times the conductor would at the point of a revolver dare the mobsters to get on his car. This [kept] up until midnight. It had gotten out of control of the police.

She continued, describing the situation as it affected the campus, where John had recently been installed as president:

Sunday night John Hope patrolled the campus—the rioters threatened to burn all of the Negro colleges. . . . [T]he responsibility [for] Morehouse [fell to] John Hope. Finally a man[,] U.S. Army on furlough[,] came over and gave Mr. Hope a gun & cartridge belt. Another teacher joined the two. They patrolled all night taking shifts. The militia came and camped at the corner and another camped at Spelman. We were not happy until we learned . . . martial law was declared. The gangsters were camping at our gates . . . and the city fathers had to send to other cities for militia and it was an out of town group at our gate. Monday we had received fire arms for protection. Friends had sent out of town for fire arms. We had enough to feel secure or rather so. It was said they came in the city in coffins. However, we had the fire arms and even though the city was under martial law, the Negroes succeeded in getting the fire arms to the people who needed them. Some were carried in soiled laundry. The Mayor gave [an] order to have Negro homes searched for fire arms. The Negroes hid their arms and also those of their neighbors who were not at home. When this order came thru—the Negroes telephoned the Governor, "take our arms and we will fire the city." That stopped the house to house inspection. The section called Darktown prepared for the mob—when the Gov. said every part of the city would be protected. The Darktown people sent word to the Gov. "Don't send the militia but send the mob." They had smothered the lights and when the mob . . . looked at those black streets, [they] were afraid and left and went off to South Atlanta where the Negroes were expecting them and there would have been blood shed—But knowing what would happen the mayor had a gatling gun hauled over the RR track and dared the mob to cross. Then he had the men in the black community arrested and of course took their arms away. We did not get the Sunday *Constitution* until about eleven o'clock. One of the department heads brought the paper and explained why he had to bring it. Told us all about the happenings of the night before. Seemed very much ashamed of the whole affair. The city streets were terrible.

John Hope got in touch with Miss Giles, Pres. of Spelman—called the Governor, asked for protection of the property of Spelman and the women on the campus. The gangsters started up to Morehouse but some of the group refused to come—They knew that [it was] a school for Negro men—& the cowards were afraid to come. Toward evening streams of women and children came up the walks. The men in the community sent the women and children to have the protection of those brick buildings while they stayed home.

In my neighborhood all of the white children were put in one of the white public schools and soldiers patrolled the school grounds. Homes were nailed up . . . —fear. These white people knew how they had treated the Negro all the while, now they feared retribution. The Negro man went home, sat in the door with his gun across his knees and was prepared to die protecting his home and family. Not until then did the good Christian white people care what happened to the Negro. But when they saw the Negro in sheer desperation decided to protect himself or die—did the churches open their doors—Fear.

No one person could have brought those people [Black Atlantans] to terms. They felt they had stood as much as any man could—They were prepared for every eventuality. So a committee was called of both races . . . with representation of [the] Negro race. They discussed [issues] man to man. The white man learned . . . in this riot . . . to get along together [with Blacks,] that there must be cooperation.[7]

Though her active local community participation extended back to her first arrival in Atlanta, the riot heightened Lugenia's civic consciousness. The plight of Black Atlanta became a stark reality to her. Race-baiting culminating in mob rule forced Black racial unity as a means of survival. Places and people associated with leadership were sought out for protection, so the college campuses became havens for people, especially women and children, seeking shelter. A woman named Mrs. Banks brought her son to the Hopes to ensure his safety while she stayed with the white family she worked for. The security of the "brick buildings" at Spelman and Atlanta Baptist colleges was reinforced not only by the presence of an armed militia made up mainly of out-of-town soldiers but moreover by the presence of armed Black men of the community—the husbands, brothers, and fathers of the families seeking safety. Lugenia recalled their strong stand on racial solidarity in their community.

Lugenia saw herself as accountable to her own West Fair neighborhood both as a community activist and as the wife of a powerful Black man. In 1906 John Hope was inaugurated as Atlanta Baptist College's first Black president, and Lugenia became the first lady of this all-male campus. In her transition from the wife of a professor to the wife of the president, her influence and prestige accelerated, but so did her duties and obligations. This new position would provide her with a different avenue to address difficult issues, but it would also bring more issues and problems to address. It would mean that those in need would expect her, Mrs. John Hope, to have immediate access to resources that would produce immediate results. People would expect her success rate to be high and her endurance long-suffering. In addition, she was to be a role model and mother figure for the student body of the college, a mother to Edward and later also to John II, and a promoter and official hostess for the school as she stood by her husband in all of his endeavors. She was to care for his home, his sons, his guests, the live-in students, and the female faculty, and she was expected to continue and expand her social activism— though the college would be her first loyalty.

Lugenia, the first lady, also inherited power. Being the president's wife would open doors previously closed or only cracked. It was a status that would bring her audiences with municipal officials who could promise, and even implement, changes in the Black community. It would bring influential memberships and leadership on a national and international basis. It would grant her a wider platform from which to continue the social reform work she had begun as Lugenia Burns. Yet there was some question whether being the first lady of Atlanta Baptist College, with all of the rights and privileges and responsibilities pertaining thereto, would stifle Lugenia Burns's spirit of independence.

As Lugenia assumed her new role on campus, her first concern was the students. Several former students remembered her as, in the words of one of them, "charming, seldom ruffled, firm, gentle, a careful thinker, and a very soft and cultured woman." Another student spoke of her as being "not the aggressive type" but "soft-spoken, a home-type person though very active in community activities." Another remembered that she would "stand on the porch, stop the students passing by, and invite them to listen to the radio, especially if something important such as a presidential address was being broadcasted." Other students felt that she "cultivated in them certain habits in dress and mannerism and set a cultural and moral tone for them." As her son Edward put it, "Dignity and self respect were fundamental aspects of her character. Money, while not to be ignored, was less important than a life of service to one's own downtrodden people. . . . Through out the College students were taught that morality, dignity, and self respect were more valuable then money or any earthly thing." Still another student recalled the "warmth in her face that invited the young men of the college to come to her to relax and tell her their problems."⁸

During the thirty-three years that Lugenia lived on the campus of Atlanta Baptist College, later Morehouse College, she tried to impart to the young men her sensitivity toward the needs of the community and the necessity of alleviating them. She encouraged students to become involved, to acquaint themselves with the low-income families nearby, and to collect toys, fruit, and food for those families at Thanksgiving, Christmas, and other holidays.⁹ Some sociology classes—those of Professors Gary Moore, Walter Chivers, and John B. Watson, for example—conducted surveys of the needs in the adjoining community for the Neighborhood Union. Once ascertained, the results were organized into a plan of action. Atlanta Baptist College and Atlanta University students joined the union in mounting special projects for the community's children. Students tutored classes in school subjects for the young children. Some conducted such industrial arts classes as woodworking and cabinetmaking. Others supervised playground activities, and still others taught Vacation Bible School during the summers and participated in intercollegiate track meets that served as fund-raisers for the union. Some of these students also worked with Lugenia in making door-to-door surveys to encourage voter registration.¹⁰

Officially, Lugenia was for many years the dormitory mother of Graves Hall. A former student and later academic dean, Brailsford Brazeal, remembered her daily room inspections: "We knew that she would be coming about nine or nine-thirty every morning. Many of us would have our doors open waiting for her." In his eulogy of Lugenia at Morehouse's memorial service in 1947, Ira de A. Reid of Atlanta University reiterated that her early days at the college were "seldom glamorous ones for she was called upon to supervise the cleaning of buildings and grounds; to keep the college accounts; and to make men out of the students."¹¹ As noted,

Lugenia also taught sculpture classes in her attic to those students of Atlanta Baptist and Spelman colleges whom she saw as gifted. During the summers she usually offered a millinery class at Spelman.

Because her own experiences had persuaded her of the value of the undertaking, Lugenia sought to establish training classes in social work, to be offered through the Neighborhood Union. In 1918 the union organized a Social Service Institute at Morehouse—a workshop of lectures on prenatal and infant care, juvenile delinquency, malnutrition, and the value of social service. Lugenia aided Professor Moore's class in organizing the three-day workshop and served as one of its faculty members. Out of this institute grew the Atlanta School of Social Work, which in 1920 became affiliated with Atlanta University.[12] Many social work students got their field experience by working with Lugenia in the union. Some served as matrons or assistants at the settlement centers; others worked in various clinics of the union; others organized recreational programs for the young children.

Lugenia was one of the founders of the still extant Morehouse Auxiliary. Organized in 1923, the auxiliary consisted of the wives of faculty and staff members united in order to enhance social life on the campus and to raise funds for the school. As a charter member, Lugenia took part in various auxiliary-sponsored functions: plays, campus-life discussions, parties, and other social affairs. The auxiliary assisted in many fund-raising campaigns by operating a snack shop in the basement of Graves Hall and holding bazaars, baby contests, and other activities that enabled it to establish scholarships and to donate a thousand dollars toward the construction of the school's first gymnasium.[13]

Lugenia's involvement with Morehouse was not limited even to this wide range of activities. Her husband is credited with organizing the first football team on campus. The team had winning seasons, and Lugenia was a team supporter. Edward recalled:

In the days before athletic scholarships, before glorified professional athletes, when the old line college sports were center stage and the little colleges such as ABC in the Negro world were just getting started, mother was in the foreground in promoting athletics. A few young players went out for the fun of it, but generally among the older students who were necessary to fill out the team since they predominated in the student body, one played football for the honor and glory of the college or not at all. I have a feeling that mother especially in the very early days helped convert some of these old timers into solid reliable football players.

She undoubtedly contributed to the collegiate atmosphere of the cheering section:

The school was a very drab, serious, hardworking place. . . . The fans, students and their guests went to the games gaily with colorful arm bands, waving bright colored pennants. So mother began making maroon and white colored pennants, cutting and sewing the letters on by hand. I doubt that mother had any financial aid but the satisfaction was in seeing the sidelines become a mass of alumni, friends, and students gaily and loyally displaying their colors.[14]

In 1929 John Hope again made history: he was inaugurated the first Black president of Atlanta University. In addition to his duties as president of Morehouse College, John now assumed the awesome task of building the first Black graduate school in the South. Atlanta University, begun in the Reconstruction era as an undergraduate institution, was now being converted to a graduate school and relocated to its current site. Former Atlanta University undergraduate students were transferred to Spelman or Morehouse colleges; after graduation, some of these students would enroll in graduate courses at Atlanta University. John at once began his drive to consolidate the organization of the Atlanta University Consortium—Morehouse College, Spelman College, and Atlanta University. He also worked to affiliate Morris Brown College, Clark University (now Clark College), and Gammon Theological Seminary. He proposed that these institutions share faculty, resources, and a library; in return, he expected these schools to improve their faculty salaries in order to attract quality teachers. Since the teachers were to be shared, he wanted all of them eligible to teach at Spelman and Morehouse. He wished to relocate Clark University, located in South Atlanta, closer to the budding intellectural center—a goal accomplished in 1942.[15]

In 1931, convinced that he had secured Morehouse's endowment, John resigned as Morehouse's leader and began to build Atlanta University. He traveled extensively to raise the necessary funds to erect a physical plant, a business administration building, a library, and the president's house.

While John was building and traveling for Atlanta University, Lugenia still lived in the president's house on the Morehouse campus. She continued to serve as first lady of the school, but she was involved little or not at all in the administration of Morehouse and the building of Atlanta University. Though she had encouraged her husband to take the university job, her participation was limited to organizing the family's move into the newly completed president's house in 1932 and planning the decoration of the house. Her community work dominated the years of John's administration at Atlanta University, as her career concentrated on the settlement projects of the Neighborhood Union. She did seek to incorporate graduate social work students into the union's community organizing and building. Just as she had secured sociology students from Morehouse over the years to assist the union's work, she now developed an alliance between the School of Social Work at the university and the union. Graduate social work majors could use the union's programs and projects to complete their required volunteer and practical works. Lugenia worked with the School of Social Work in organizing programs to bring the school and the neighborhood of West Fair closer together. For example, Atlanta University social work students assisted the union with its unemployment program in the West Fair area during the depression. Soup kitchens, clothing drives, and temporary shelters were provided as relief for needy families.[16] Lugenia also worked for slum clearance in the Beaver Slide area. She and her husband, and other members of the union, agreed to sell the union's property on West Fair Street when the federal government promised to build public housing for the Black community. Thus University Homes became one of the earliest public housing projects for Blacks in the country. In these ways Mrs. First Lady of Atlanta University continued her public life, extending it even more deeply into the community around her than she had done during her Morehouse years.

In 1933 the Neighborhood Union celebrated its twenty-fifth anniversary and hosted an appreciation banquet for its founder, Lugenia Burns Hope. Two years later Lugenia retired from the union, though she remained active on a national level. Also in 1935 she participated in the founding session of the National Council of Negro Women, led by Mary McLeod Bethune. She made lecture tours, she was an official in the clubwomen's movement, she participated in the interracial movement in the South, and she served as an officer in the local branch of the NAACP. All of these positions called for her to travel. Yet she and John rarely undertook trips together during this period, though they had done so in earlier years. When their sons were home, as noted in the preceding chapter, both parents tried not to be away at the same time. Both were concerned that their sons not feel neglected, and when both were at home, family events were important. The sons remembered that their parents always worked together as a team, "an unbeatable team with each zealously attempting to encourage and assist the other."[17]

Even after the children were grown and away and after John's health began to fail, however, he still traveled on business and leisure without Lugenia. Once, while recuperating from a major illness, he took his secretary with him (upon his family's insistence), but not his wife. John's physician seems to have recommended travel for him as the best route back to health: being away from Atlanta and his work would speed up a complete recovery. Later, following a serious illness in 1933, John lived for several months in MacVicar Hospital on Spelman's campus. He now lived, traveled, and worked without his wife.

Though Lugenia, too, had periods of poor health, she still traveled for her causes. One of the few recorded trips they made together after 1920 was to the dedication of a building on the campus of Bethune-Cookman in Florida—they were both close to Mary McLeod Bethune, founder of the college— and then on to a brief vacation in Nassau.[18] John vacationed in the Caribbean, South America, the Canal Zone, and Europe, all without Lugenia. While he wrote her lengthy letters during these trips, as he had done in the past, still they were not together. Other than decorating the presidential house and supervising the construction and design of the family home in north Georgia in 1934, Lugenia was left mostly with her social and women's work. Did she, one wonders, understand and accept this constant absence of her husband, or did she remain behind because she wished to be alone?

Lugenia certainly did understand the demands for her husband's speeches and appearances. To the president of a Black college and university, fund-raising was always critical, and it was especially vital during the Booker T. Washington era, when private Black liberal arts schools were generally excluded from the donations of northern philanthropists. Further, both Hopes were vocal integrationists who fought constantly for full equality and citizenship for Black people. John was the only Black college president at the commencement of the Niagara Movement in 1905 and one of the earliest supporters of the NAACP. Because of their recognition as race persons, both John and Lugenia were expected to contribute when asked; during World War I, for instance, John worked with the YMCA while Lugenia ran the Black hostess-house program for the YWCA. Yet although both of them had busy lives outside the home, Lugenia still had domestic responsibilities, supervising her household and her children and providing support for her husband. When John was away, he wrote her detailed accounts of his activities, desires, beliefs, successes, and failures, soliciting her support, insight, evaluations, love, and patience. His letters called up her every energy. Not only, then, did she miss his presence, but his letters were not always strong sources of encouragement.

At one time or another, both of the Hopes believed that they were neglecting each other. John wrote her in 1920 and often thereafter about missing her on his trips, even after most of them no longer included her. He wrote passionate letters, recollecting some spot they had visited together and the romantic time they had shared there. Yet his constant declarations of love could not and did not shelter her from numerous rumors of his infidelity, especially with white women. She was aware of the allegations that her husband was a ladies' man, and she addressed them in dealing with his biographer, Ridgely Torrence: "Some white women were aggressive. But he paid no attention to that. He was a southeman [southern gentleman] and treated all women with the greatest respect." Then she warned him: "Don't let the few stories that you may hear color the life of the man—because the book would be FALSE. The associations were simply CASUAL OR IN-CIDENTAL IN HIS LIFE." She challenged the biographer to "write as much of the truth as you can absorb."[19] Torrence chose not to touch this part of his subject's life.

Still Lugenia loved her Jack. Her family was essential to her. To diffuse the tensions, she concentrated even more of her energies into her work. The volume of the workload increased, and so did the trips. She allowed herself to be involved in increasing numbers of projects. The workload and the absence from home caused guilt and conflict, and her husband's absence caused stress and loneliness, but Lugenia channeled these emotions into her work. This decision was a conscious one, for this controlled and determined person could not allow herself to tolerate the idea of succumbing to a personal crisis. Just as she expected to be always in control of her home, the union, the campus, and the students, so this was to be the pattern in her marriage. To acknowledge anything like pain, mistrust, or betrayal would contradict this established firmness. She kept herself too busy being needed away from home, going and doing, to confront any personal anguish, even in her most private written thoughts. Maybe for her, race leaders, especially strong Black women, the torchbearers, the Harriet Tubmans and the Sojourner Truths, had no choice of being anything but strong. As she now began to internalize her personal turmoil, Lugenia less often showed herself as lively and fun-loving. She grew somewhat austere, even at times distant, while she gave more play to the dominating and assertive capacities that made her a natural leader. She began, indeed, to organize and structure her life around her public role as Mrs. John Hope.

This status as the wife of a university president opened many doors and gave her instant recognition and acceptance. It provided her with opportunities for leadership, which brought power. That she enjoyed her power and had a natural talent for execution is well illustrated by her continued control over the Neighborhood Union for twenty-five years, regardless of the actual elected leadership.

Lugenia's focus on race reform reflects the ways in which Black women in prestigious positions often did not merely enjoy the perquisites of their positions but instead sought to use them to influence change in their communities. Like Lugenia, many other first ladies at predominantly Black institutions were members of the southern caucus of the Commission on Interracial Cooperation, the YWCA, the NAACP, and the Southeastern Federation of Colored Women's Clubs. On a local level they organized settlement houses, reading rooms, and medical clinics for the needy. The names begin to repeat themselves in the literature: Mary Jackson McCrorey, Johnson C. Smith (formerly Biddle) University, Charlotte, North Carolina; Florence Hunt, Fort Valley State College, Fort Valley, Georgia; Marion B. Wilkinson, South Carolina State College, Orangeburg; Margaret Murray Washington and Jennie Moton, both of Tuskegee Institute (now Tuskegee University), Tuskegee, Alabama; Julia A. Fountain, Morris Brown College, Atlanta; and A. Vera Davage, Clark College, Atlanta.

Membership in this southern network offered Lugenia a forum for recognition as a woman, not as a wife, mother, or first lady, even though the latter status may have brought her into the network. It gave her a chance to express her views on woman suffrage, racial oppression, and sexual discrimination (both intraracial and interracial); it brought her international solidarity with women of color; and it opened the opportunity to share strategies on organizing and reforming. Usually viewed as a radical who demanded immediate justice, who was less patient with accommodationist approaches to racial or feminist issues than her peers, Lugenia was often misunderstood. Yet she vocalized the frustrations felt even by those who were less liberated.

In conjunction with their work on civic, social, and racial uplift projects, many of these first ladies of Black colleges taught or directed programs at their respective institutions. Margaret M. Washington was the director of Girls' Industries and dean of women at Tuskegee Institute; she was succeeded as dean of women by Jennie Moton. Mary J. McCrorey taught psychology, education, English, and secretarial work at Johnson C. Smith. Lugenia, although she was not involved in education to the same extent, taught sculpture and millinery classes, while serving as bookkeeper and dormitory inspector.[20]

Lugenia's ties to Morehouse and Atlanta University—she spent thirty-three years at the former and four at the latter—were strong even if not primarily academic. These were years that saw her gain national and international recognition as a public reform activist, years in which she watched the Neighborhood Union become more than a local reality. Neither the status she attained nor the associated duties affected her loyalty to the student bodies, the administrations, her two homes, her sons, and her husband. Recognition did not change her love for Morehouse or the student body. It did not deflect her efforts to unite the local neighborhood reform efforts with the graduate social work program of Atlanta University. It did not deter her from raising her sons, promoting her husband's career, or conducting her protocol duties as the college president's wife on two campuses. Mostly, this public life satisfied her desire to be needed and validated her existence to herself, even as it addressed urgent needs in the community around her. As she gained prominence for her talents in community building and racial activism, it became apparent that what had begun many years before in Chicago during her adolescence had matured into a lifelong mission.

Chapter Four

"Thy Neighbor as Thyself": The Neighborhood Union, 1908–1936

By the turn of the century Atlanta was the most segregated city in Georgia. As early as 1890 Atlanta had instituted Jim Crow laws that separated the city into distinctive Black and white areas. These discriminatory laws reinforced white supremacy by excluding Blacks from public accommodations, by establishing residential ordinances that restricted the living patterns of Blacks and contributed directly to Atlanta's neglect of blighted areas, by exposing Black customers to shabby treatment when they entered downtown stores, and by excluding Blacks from political participation and denying them due process of law.[1]

Segregation worked in Atlanta as long as Blacks obeyed these laws and as long as they were kept subordinate. Segregation was legal; opposition meant breaking the law.[2] Violence was considered acceptable when necessary to maintain the status quo, as in Atlanta's race riot of 1906.

In 1900 Atlanta's city fathers instituted the white primary "on the grounds that Black participation corrupted local politics." Atlanta, a bulwark of democratic rule, feared the return of the Black voter to the polls. In the past, disgruntled whites had used Black voters to decide conflicts between two or more white candidates during general elections, rounding up eligible Blacks, bribing them, and wagoning them to the polls for the Democratic ticket. Though unscrupulous politicians used alcohol and money to purchase votes, it was the voters exclusively who were judged corruptible. So in 1908, under the tutelage of Hoke Smith, Georgia adopted disfranchisement laws. Even though Black voters were dramatically reduced, these laws and the white primary did not apply to most general, open, or special municipal elections; further, some liberal whites and Black leaders organized an interracial committee to promote racial harmony. Nonetheless, race relations in Atlanta in the early 1900s had reached their "nadir."[3]

Atlanta's Black community numbered sixty-three thousand by 1900. Most lived in varied pockets throughout the city. The Fourth Ward and Auburn Avenue had for some time housed the older Black Atlantans who composed the city's Black aristocracy. Mainly of mulatto ancestry, this upper class consisted of entrepreneurs and businesspeople whose clientele was predominantly white. By 1900 a new group of Blacks, mostly in-migrants to Atlanta, made up this professional and business group. This new group of professionals never accounted for more than 4 percent of the population, however, for the majority of Black Atlantans were poor residents who lived in slum areas with dilapidated houses and schools and who were mainly unskilled or semiskilled laborers. The women worked in domestic and personal services. Urban employers usually hired Black men only for the duration of a particular construction project or contract. As Jacqueline Jones has noted, "These sporadic wage-earning opportunities guaranteed . . . low wages and long periods of enforced idleness." So Black women became the breadwinners of their families, working in white households, as laundresses and washerwomen, and as sellers of vegetables, fruits, and flowers. Women of the upper and middle classes were generally seamstresses and schoolteachers. (The latter became the promoters of racial consciousness and the organizers of women's clubs.)[4]

Black Atlanta also had a notable artisan class that dominated brickmasonry, carpentry, and barbering, yet by 1900 these skilled laborers had lost their positions and patronage to white laborers. Throughout the South, management used Blacks as strikebreakers to destroy the union movement. White employers who hired Blacks, even in menial capacities, were forced by white employees to fire all of the Black employees and to replace them with whites. White workers even struck to maintain white supremacy. In those industries where Black women were retained—for example, some tobacco factories in North Carolina—whites demanded that they be segregated.[5]

The twentieth century also ushered in the Progressive Era, with its championship of social justice and municipal reforms. While sexual and racial equalities were agenda items in some parts of Progressive America, in Georgia Progressivism was conservative, racist, and elitist. Throughout the state, Blacks were routinely denied basic city services, whether the municipal government was corrupt or honest, reformist or reactionary. In Atlanta, Progressivism was for whites only; Blacks were either excluded or attacked outright. White Atlantans, arguing that Blacks corrupted the political process, endorsed their disfranchisement as a method of cleaning up the government. Progressives in Atlanta pushed prohibition so that liquor would be unavailable as a means of buying votes in "wet" areas. They called for the end of the convict-lease system in Georgia, pointing to the 10 percent of convicts who were white in order to solicit public support, even though 90 percent of the victims were Black; Progressives argued for the chain gang as a humanitarian substitute. Progressives campaigned for compulsory education bills in Atlanta in order to force white children to attend school. Too many educated Blacks, on the other hand, threatened white supremacy. Southern suffragists supported the Nineteenth Amendment only if it guaranteed that Black men and women would be disfranchised; thus this amendment did not benefit Black Georgians at all. The Progressive Movement, which could have united all reformers, instead became a major component in maintaining white supremacy and solidarity and Black subordination and intimidation. Black Atlantans therefore turned inward, using their organizations, churches, businesses, fraternal lodges, literary groups, women's clubs, and colleges to meet social, economic, medical, educational, recreational, and civic needs.[6]

Around the turn of the century, Atlanta's Black communities tended to congregate in six major sections and a number of smaller ones. These communities were usually named after some activity, person, or physical feature associated with the area: Tanyard Bottom; Reynoldstown (named for Joseph Reynolds, a Black man who was the area's first settler); Beaver Slide. Living conditions in these areas were deplorable: inadequate sanitation, lighting, sewage disposal, and housing contributed to neighborhood crime and vice. Health conditions were far below the norm for white Atlanta, with Blacks succumbing particularly often to consumption and pneumonia. The overall death rate for Blacks was approximately 150% higher than for whites. Nevertheless, some of these communities were found to be secure places during such crises as riots, fires, and epidemics; one scholar of Black Atlanta has described them as "cities of refuge, cities of brotherhood."[7]

The West Side district was bordered by Beckwith Street on the north, Green's Ferry Street on the south, Ashby Street on the west, and Walnut Street on the east. Ghetto areas of the district included Beaver Slide, the West Fair Street Bottom, and Battle's Alley, also known as "the bottom." Dens of vice, houses of prostitution, hovels, outdoor toilets and shotgun houses mingled with

Major Black Areas of Atlanta, ca. 1900

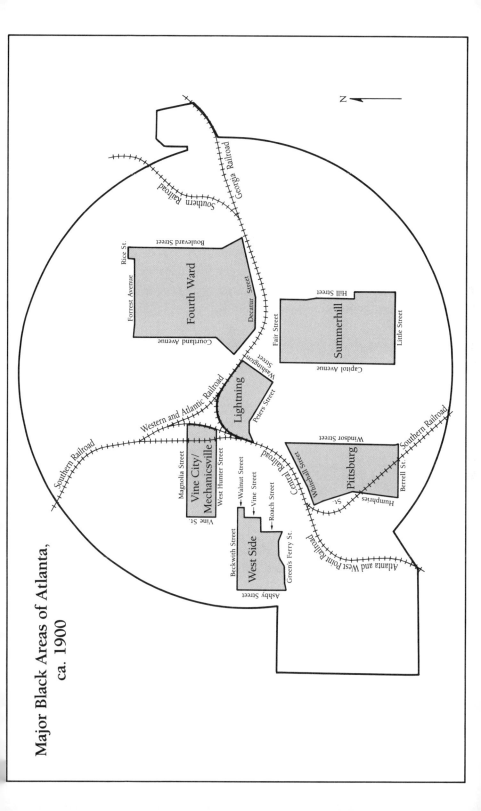

N

Southern Railroad

Georgia Railroad

Rice St.

Boulevard Street

Forrest Avenue

Fourth Ward

Decatur Street

Courtland Avenue

Hill Street

Fair Street

Summerhill

Capitol Avenue

Little Street

Washington Street

Lightning

Peters Street

Western and Atlantic Railroad

Southern Railroad

Magnolia Street

Vine City/ Mechanicsville

West Hunter Street

Vine St.

Walnut Street

Vine Street

Roach Street

Central Railroad

Windsor Street

Whitehall Street

Pittsburg

St.

Humphries

Berrell St.

Southern Railroad

Beckwith Street

West Side

Ashby Street

Green's Ferry St.

Atlanta and West Point Railroad

some older homes of whites. White's Alley, Peters Street, and Roach Street, where brawls, shootings, cuttings, gambling, and killings were all-too-frequent occurrences, terrified the neighborhood children. Beckwith Street, Atlanta University's southern boundary, was full of hills, holes, mud, and rocks, and the city unloaded rubbish there in an effort to level it. Between Beckwith and Fair streets the city dumped and burned its garbage, and in the midst of this area were shanty dwellings where poor Blacks lived. Chestnut Street (now James P. Brawley Drive) was developed by whites who were later replaced by graduates of Atlanta University and Spelman and Morehouse colleges. Still, there were no water mains, and the smoke and stench from nearby disposal areas made sleeping difficult for the residents.[8]

East of Atlanta University was a similar district called Vine City or Mechanicsville, where slums, dumps, hovels, crime, and deprivation prevailed. Directly adjacent was the section known as Lightning, which was the backwash of Peters and West Mitchell streets. This region was "considered the number one slum area," and "it was here that the city permitted houses of prostitution."[9] As in other Black sections, the houses and streets were in bad condition.

In Summerhill, a section on the city's southeast side, most of the Black residents owned small pieces of unimproved property. Summerhill was bordered on the east by Hill Street, on the west by Capitol Avenue, on the south by Little Street, and on the north by Fair Street. In the early history of Atlanta this area had been the city's dumping ground. Although Blacks owned most of the homes and businesses here, they were not able to get lights, water, sewage disposal, or pavement.[10]

West of Summerhill was Pittsburg, built around the Southern Railroad system: from Humphries Street on the west, to Windsor Street on the east, to Berrell Street on the south, to Whitehall Street on the north. The inhabitants of Pittsburg were well-paid railway shop workers, skilled laborers, plasterers, cement finishers, and domestics. Like other Black sections, Pittsburg had its poolrooms and churches, drugstores and upholstery shops. The poorest area was "Tin Can Alley," where the city had dumped heaps of old rusty tin and debris to fill up the gullies. Crime was prevalent here as in other Black neighborhoods. The school in the community was a patchwork of sheds built one against another from odds and ends that had been given by a wealthy Black Realtor and other people.[11]

The Fourth Ward section was regarded as the best residential section for Blacks. It was bounded by Decatur Street on the south, Courtland Avenue on the west, Boulevard Street on the east, and Forrest Avenue on the north. But it had its less attractive elements: Decatur Street housed the city jail and recorder, courthouse, dens of vice, slums, pawnshops, poolrooms, bars, cheap eating places, and theaters. There were Jewish second-hand shops, as well as Produce Row, the heart of the wholesale food market for the South. Auburn Avenue held the majority of the Black businesses. As in the other Black sections, the schools were inadequate and dilapidated, and the children played in an area where vice was rampant. Darktown, a slum area of this section, consisted of one-story wooden dwellings packed closely together.[13]

Outside the city limit, Brownsville, in South Atlanta, was surrounded by Clark University and Gammon Theological Seminary. Many of the residents were artisans and owners of attractive, well-furnished homes. Between 1890 and 1930 Brownsville emerged as one of the "cities of refuge," a status particularly noticeable during the Atlanta riot of 1906. Favorable conditions in the community deteriorated, however, when Clark University (now Clark College) moved to the west side of Atlanta in 1942.[12]

Other, smaller Black communities dotted the city. Tanyard Bottom, northeast of the West Side, was the site of the city's oldest tannery. Reynoldstown was a small Black railroad community built around the railroad shops of the Georgia and Western on the eastern edge of the city. Adjacent to the northern, middle-class white community of Buckhead were Macedonia Park and Johnsontown, which provided Buckhead's domestics. Plunket Town, on the southern periphery of Atlanta, was distinguished by a complete lack of sewer lines. Lynwood Park was situated near Oglethorpe University, and its residents worked at the school. Edgewood, or East Atlanta, was populated mostly by domestics and landscape gardeners. Still other Black areas were Peoplestown and Thomasville.[14]

As noted above, within all of these areas substandard living conditions prevailed. Generally the streets were heaped with rubbish and garbage; the homes and schools were inferior; and health facilities were totally lacking. Neighborhoods became segregated ghettos. Law enforcement was negligible. Dives, saloons, alcohol, morphine, and cocaine provided emotional escapes and led to crime and community problems.[15]

Legal segregation and Jim Crowism served as cohesive forces for Black communities throughout the South and provided at least part of the impetus that encouraged Black Atlantans, like other Black southerners, to begin building their own socioeconomic foundations. Social services were provided by churches, benevolent and fraternal societies, schools and universities, and neighborhood businesses. For example, the First Congregational Church provided a gymnasium—as early as 1875, when there was no YWCA or YMCA for young Black Atlantans—a shelter for homeless girls, an employment bureau, day nurseries, prison missions, and classes in domestic science and industrial classes for the blind.[16] It was a continuation of this sense of community responsibility that led to the establishment of social welfare agencies. Indeed, this was the case with the founding of Atlanta's Neighborhood Union.

Though deplorable living conditions for Blacks in Atlanta were stimulus enough to unite neighborhoods and to spark them into action, the specific incident that led to the Neighborhood Union's development was the death of a young woman in the community immediately surrounding the college campuses on the West Side. Louie D. Shivery, for many years the union's corresponding secretary, recorded the chilling tragedy in her study of organized social work among Black Atlantans. A young couple and the wife's father moved into the community. The husband and father worked, and the wife remained home. Because of her personality and general disposition, the woman did not make friends easily. Shivery tells what happened:

> She was taken sick and the two men not thinking her case was serious, went each morning to their work. After a few days, some of the more thoughtful neighbors, not having seen this woman about, called and found her very ill and greatly in need of care. They did what they could for her comfort, but in a few hours she died. Deeply grieving that at their very door and under the shadow of [Morehouse] College, a poor woman could sicken and die probably for the want of such womanly care as the neighbors could have given had they known the College women said, "this should not be; we should know our neighbors better."[17]

Lugenia, who learned about the tragedy soon afterward, saw the opportunity to organize the community. The incident had occurred, she believed, because of the absence of neighborly feelings.[18] The result was a meeting of the neighbors and the development of an organization.

On Thursday evening, July 8, 1908, Lugenia called a meeting of her neighbors to discuss "whether those assembled thought it needful to have settlement work in the community, and to solicit their cooperation." The idea was accepted; those in attendance believed that such work would benefit the neighborhood. The women decided to develop an organization whose objective would be the "moral, social, intellectual, and religious uplift of the community and the neighborhood in which the organization or its branches may be established." They elected Lugenia president, Hattie Watson secretary, and Dora Whitaker treasurer. Their target area, they decided, would be the immediate community, bounded by the streets Ashby, Walnut, Green's Ferry, and Beckwith. This section was designated a district and divided into subsections. Participants in the new organization were asked to visit families on the streets assigned and to bring back to the next meeting the names of the parents and children, especially the names of girls between the ages of eight and twenty-two.[19]

Reports returned to the union at its second meeting showed that there were major needs in the area that no one, including the city, was working to alleviate. Attendance at this second meeting was double that at the first. The women voted to name their group the Neighborhood Union, to adopt "Thy Neighbor as Thyself" for their motto, and to raise "the standard of living in the community and to make the West Side of Atlanta a better place to rear our children."[20]

Aided by students of Morehouse, the union conducted house-to-house surveys in order to introduce the organization to the community. Union members canvassed one hundred families around the college, informing the residents that their purpose was to organize and to provide for the children of the area. The union stressed the welfare of children over that of adults: the children were viewed as future citizens, and measures taken on their behalf were to be preventive rather than remedial. The union intended to provide services needed by the community until a permanent agency—whether city, state, or federal—was developed to take over the work.[21]

The survey disclosed that streets were in need of improvement, that lighting was insufficient, that there were few if any sewage facilities, that the water supply was mainly from surface wells (which were uncovered and thus hazardous to children), that juvenile delinquency and houses of ill repute were present, that school buildings were dilapidated and inadequate, that garbage was seldom collected and never covered, that unscreened surface toilets were common, that housing (even that under construction) was poor, that there were no recreational areas, and that families experienced a great deal of disorganization. These results were reported to the union members at the July 23 meeting. In order to attack the evils of the community "to which the boys and girls were exposed," the members defined for themselves a number of lofty aims: to provide playgrounds, clubs, and neighborhood centers for physical, moral, and intellectual development; to develop a spirit of helpfulness among neighbors; to establish lecture courses for the purpose of encouraging habits of cleanliness; to promote child welfare; to impart a sense of cultural heritage; to abolish slums and houses of immorality; to improve the sanitation of homes and streets; to bring about efficiency in general homemaking; to cooperate with the Associated Charities and the Juvenile Court; and to cooperate with city officials in suppressing vice and crime. The ultimate goal of the union was to organize neighborhoods in each section of the city and establish settlement houses in each neighborhood, where the "people could gather for their meetings, clubs and classes and feel that they were their very own."[22]

To implement these goals, the union divided the city into zones; with each zone under a chairperson elected by the neighborhood. The zones were further divided into neighborhoods and the neighborhoods into districts. Each district was supervised by a neighborhood president, whose duty it was to organize the neighborhood and to preserve records for the union, and by a director chosen from among the key women who had aided the union during its initial survey. Directors were required to conduct house-to-house surveys and visits to acquaint their districts with the plan for neighborhood improvement, relief, and solidarity. Familiarity with the economic and social status of her district's residents was of course essential for each director. The findings of the neighborhood president and the director were reported back to the union.

The directors of the districts were organized into a Board of Directors, of which the president of the Neighborhood Union was chairperson. The work of the city as a whole was to be supervised by the Board of Managers, consisting of zone chairpersons, department heads, and presidents of the various neighborhood branches. This board was the governing force, with the power to appoint committees that conducted other aspects of the union's work and to set up additional branches in other localities. This board was also required to make annual reports to the members of the union. By 1911, the year of the union's incorporation, it had expanded beyond the West Side into four additional communities: Pittsburg, Summerhill, the Fourth Ward, and South Atlanta. By 1914 branches were established throughout the city.[23]

Membership was open to all members of "worthy" families within a given branch's boundaries who would organize under its direction. The membership fee was set at ten cents per month per family, but moneys for the work of the union came mainly from donations and fund-raisers like carnivals, apron sales, bake sales, baseball games, track meets, and bridge tournaments. When the union became a member of the Community Chest in 1924, its annual budget of five thousand dollars gained a monthly subsidy of twenty-five dollars; a year later, however, the union was dropped from the larger organization in an economy move.

Under Lugenia's leadership, the union was divided into four departments. The Moral and Educational Department sponsored lectures, special meetings, and a large number of projects; the

Literary Department secured good books; the Musical Department cultivated a love for good music, particularly Black music; and the Arts Department secured teachers and materials for classes, made out schedules, and arranged the work.

The Arts Department recruited teachers from Morehouse, Spelman, Atlanta University, and Tuskegee Institute (and student teachers from Morehouse) to offer classes in sewing, cooking, basketry, embroidery, woodworking, millinery (taught by Lugenia), textiles, food preparation, gardening and yard beautification, folk dancing, housecleaning, storytelling and song, dressmaking, pattern drafting, and fitting. At the time the union was founded the city's public schools offered no vocational classes for Black boys and girls. These classes offered by the union were therefore vigorously promoted until the schools added vocational classes to their curricula.

Clubs, including reading and painting circles, were established through the relevant departments for boys and girls between the ages of eight and twenty-two. Union members believed that "wholesome recreation and cultural education" were essential "for the people of the community," and parents were taught to "entertain their children in order to keep them off the streets." Specific entertainments and activities were planned for older girls. Young male teachers instructed the neighborhood boys in manual training, military tactics, and athletics. Student dues of ten cents a month were instituted to cover the costs of these programs.[24]

Much of the work of the union fell under the auspices of the Moral and Education Department. One of its functions was to sponsor public gatherings to "arouse group mindedness and to secure cooperation through lectures and mass meetings."[25] Lectures by people of national reputation, like Margaret Murray Washington and Mary McLeod Bethune, covered topics in health, morals, education, citizenship, child welfare, and general culture.

Each member was asked to serve on several of the standing

committees into which this department was subdivided: Investigation, Finance, Health, Fundraising, Publicity, Child Welfare, Religion, Children's Club, Relief, Cooperation, Recreation and Entertainment, Improvement, Sanitary, Visiting, and Civics. The most impressive was the Investigation Committee. Priding themselves on improving the moral fiber of their communities, the women who made up this committee charged themselves with investigating and reporting to the union "everything that seems to be a menace to our neighborhood." Records from various meetings show that this committee reported to the directors both women and houses of questionable character. Where there were members who could share firsthand insight, their comments were solicited. From these reports the union drew up in each instance a petition of removal, presented to the director of the affected district for the necessary signatures and then forwarded to the mayor. The petition identified the woman, her address, and those activities that made her detrimental to the community. The signatures affixed commanded the mayor to act swiftly in removing the undesirable(s). That results were produced is reflected in the minutes of two specific meetings:

February 1911 Minutes:
Mrs. Barnett succeeded in getting two families out of her district who indulged in doing things that were immoral such as breaking the Sabbath and gambling.

August 8, 1912 Minutes:
The Mildred Street Case has been satisfactorily disposed of. The Holy Rollers were made to move on the grounds of disorderly conduct.[26]

So the moral cleanup of the community meant the removal of what the neighborhood women saw as unsavory elements. Their concerns centered around the young girls, whom they felt responsible for saving from the influence of these "fallen" women.

As early as the 1908 surveys, the union began confronting the city of Atlanta with the urgent needs it was uncovering. Union members petitioned the mayor, the City Council, and the Sanitation and Health departments to improve facilities. They went to court to ask for better health and housing programs, better streets, and more streetlights to prevent crime. They approached individual councilmen, trying to win their goodwill. As a result, the city welfare worker, Phillip Weltner, invited a committee from the union to meet with City Hall to discuss common problems. He then asked the committee to coordinate the union's settlement work with the city's. Later the city turned over to the union all of the settlement work for Blacks in Atlanta.[27]

Providing recreational centers and a health care program were among other important early efforts of the union. As noted, the first playground for the city's Black children was donated by Atlanta Baptist College. Later Spelman donated a plot for supervised play. These lots soon filled, and the union members began to use vacant lots as supervised play areas.

The union offered classes in nursing, home hygiene, bathing the sick, prenatal care, and infant care. Instructions were disseminated on the identification and treatment of hookworm, typhoid, pellagra, and tuberculosis. The first clinics set up were for adults, but as the adults became more responsible for their health needs the union's attention turned increasingly to the children. Monthly mothers' meetings taught facts about tuberculosis and their children's need for medical care. A group of lectures on teeth and their care led to the establishment of an ongoing dental clinic for the children. Infant and preschool children's clinics were set up as well. At the Anti-Tuberculosis Clinic, patients were referred to specific physicians. Volunteer nurses and doctors visited homes, clubs, and churches. The union's report for July 1910 stated that over 135 such visits had been made, and "the 'follow up' work of this clinic will show that 99% of those patients have followed the instructions given them at the Neighborhood Union Clinic this month."28

During the year in which the union was receiving funding from the Community Chest the union mounted a successful fund-raising campaign for its health program, prompting Roy Gates of the Community Chest to protest that the campaign was hurting both organizations. Gates informed the union that the Community Chest had surveyed the health conditions of the city and that its intention was to turn the "colored" health drive over to the union. The women of the Neighborhood Union decided to acquiesce. In segregated Atlanta there was really very little else they could do. Protest would only lose them the support of the Community Chest, and after all, minute as those funds were, they were needed. Because the children's welfare was the first priority, the union accepted a restricted health program under Community Chest auspices. By 1925, however, Community Chest funding had been dropped anyway. Thereafter the union's health programs were run independently.29

The first union health clinic location was a house at the corner of West Fair and Mildred Streets, purchased from a friend of one of the members on October 14, 1908. Funds raised from bake sales and donations were used to make a partial payment. Soon this property was sold and plans were made to acquire a permanent structure. The union then bought property on Lee Street, later selling it for $1,500. In June 1914 the union purchased the property at 41 Leonard Street from Spelman and opened a center. The Woman's American Baptist Home Mission Society appropriated a monthly salary for a matron, and the union hired Carrie Bell Cole from New York. In its first year the center served over four hundred patients. The center operated successfully at this location until 1926, when the Leonard Street property was sold to the Leonard Street Orphanage and the union purchased a lot on West Fair Street.

In 1926, under the supervision of Ludie Andrews, a registered nurse and the Neighborhood Union's president, the union opened its new Health Center at 706 West Fair Street. The opening was a grand event: Margaret Murray Washington dedicated the building and poet Georgia Douglass Johnson delivered the main address. The union operated at this location until 1934, when the federal government offered to purchase the lot to build federal housing for Blacks. The government offered $5,370 for the property and guaranteed to build a center for the union in the housing project. The union's rental fee was approximately 4 percent of the cost of the property. Repairs and security—a hired watchman—for the new center were to be provided by the government. The Executive Committee of the union agreed to sell the property in order to aid governmental efforts at slum clearance. Following necessary expenditures, the balance was deposited in the Citizen's Trust Company, the local Black-owned bank, and the new center was opened.[30]

At the dedication of University Homes, Harold L. Ickes, secretary of the interior, praised the residents' thorough organization and their "systematic work towards the improvement of the housing conditions over a long period of years." The union's secretary recorded this as a historic acknowledgment of the union, which was the one organization in the West Fair area that had worked for

> twenty-five years to improve living conditions among blacks, taking its fight to city council, to churches, and finally to the real estate agents, themselves, through a survey of their property. Hence, the Neighborhood Union is due the credit . . . for the choosing of the Federal Government of the Beaver Slide Slum District for its first national housing project.[31]

From its inception, members of the Neighborhood Union had agreed that an essential goal of the organization would be the welfare of the children of the area. Programs designed to provide services and facilities for the children were begun at once. Yet paramount for the members was the quality of education these children were receiving in the Black public schools of Atlanta. In 1913 the union began an investigation of the city's Black schools. The Women's Civic and Social Improvement Committee, chaired by Lugenia, was organized "to investigate conditions with a view of remedying the evils." To substantiate the handicaps that resulted from operating the schools in double sessions, the committee received from each school principal the names and addresses of absentees from their schools during a particular month. Members secured a list of responsible parents, who testified that their children's health was impaired by crowded conditions in the public schools. Physicians gave an estimate of the extent of ill health among teachers owing to overwork and poor conditions in the schools. Churches gave estimates of the number of children who could not enter school because of the limited seating capacity.[32]

For six months this committee of "one hundred leading women of Atlanta" investigated and inspected the twelve Black schools in the city. Overall conditions were found deplorable: sanitary conditions were unhealthy; lighting and ventilation were unusually poor, with many children consequently suffering eyestrain and sickness; classrooms were crowded; and there were double sessions with the same teacher for both sessions. For the year 1913–14, there was a seating capacity in the Black schools of 4,102 but an enrollment of 6,163, so that the number of pupils served by each double session was around 3,081.[33]

The committee contacted every influential white woman in the city, including members of the Board of Lady Visitors of the Board of Education, soliciting their support. Some of these white women visited the schools and saw at first hand the actual conditions. The committee also interviewed each member of the City Council, the mayor, the members of the Board of Education, Black ministers, members of Black women's clubs, and members of other Black organizations. They solicited help from influential Black men (including their husbands). Committee members spoke before Black congregations, explaining the nature of their project and urging parents to pay their personal taxes and to have their children vaccinated. The committee reached other members of the community by persuading insurance agents to inform their clients of the committee's work as they made their collections. Using newspapers and mass meetings, the committee publicized the deplorable conditions it had discovered by its surveys. Pictures of these conditions were published in local newspapers.

The women were given permission by the Board of Education to have a committee of six at each school on the first day of the term to collect the names and addresses of those children who had not been vaccinated. The members then visited the children's parents and saw to it that the children were vaccinated and returned to school the following school day. The women kept up a running campaign for better conditions, posting placards and giving illustrated lectures to show the problems. They drew up a petition to attack the inadequacies of the schools and forwarded it to the Board of Education:

Gentlemen:—

We, a committee of women representing residents and tax-payers of the city of Atlanta upon visiting and making a careful inspection of the public schools for Negroes, find most of them in a very unsanitary condition. The lighting capacity in many instances is insufficient, the playgrounds small as compared to the seating capacity of the buildings. For a number of years the overcrowded condition of the schools in the four or five lower grades has resulted in double sessions in those grades, in lieu of additional buildings, and the continuous increase of the populations has resulted in the use of annexes. These annexes fall far below the condition necessary to effectual work by the teachers, and by the pupils.

In view of these conditions, we hereby respectfully beg leave to present, in interest of the civic and social welfare of our Negro boys and girls of Atlanta, this petition, asking that your honorable body at the earliest time practical effect changes relative to the following.

First, Sanitary Conditions. We find unhealthful conditions existing in all of our public schools except in Yonge Street School, and in Gray Street School. We wish to call especial attention to the schools mentioned below: Houston, Mitchell, Pittsburg, and L & N. At the Houston St. School the condition of the toilets is such as to impair the health of all concerned. We believe that this condition is due to the fact that the toilets are too small to accommodate the large number of children.

At Pittsburg and at Mitchell Street Schools the toilet arrangements are indecent and tend to immorality, in that only a wooden partition separates that section . . . used by the boys from that section used by the girls. In many schools, especially in the Summerhill and L & N schools, the walls are in a deplorable condition. The basement room in daily use for the first and second grade[s] at Roach Street School necessitates artificial light on dark days, and is so damp as to injure the health of the children.

Second, A school in South Atlanta. South Atlanta, with its hundreds of children who are of school age, and whose parents are tax payers is without a school.

Third, Feeble-minded children. We beg that special provision be made for the feeble-minded and the defective children.

Fourth, Double Sessions. We urge the Board's prayerful consideration of abolishing the system of double sessions. We find that under the existing system three hours and a half are devoted to a set of children for work outlined for a five hour schedule. This, we maintain, is conducive to poor scholarship in grammar school subjects. We believe that the double session enforces idleness, and thereby promotes shiftlessness in our children. Employers can not use help in the morning during one month, and in the afternoon during the next month. The majority of the parents are in service and their children being unemployed are on the streets out of school hours. We hold that children who attend the afternoon session, do so at a great disadvantage. A teacher who has taught from forty to sixty children in the morning can not properly teach another set of children in the afternoon. Another evil of the system of double sessions is evidenced in the impaired health of teachers.

It is for this, then, that we beg of you: better sanitary conditions in our public schools; a school for So. Atlanta; provision for the feebleminded and for the defective children; and the abolishing of the system of double sessions. We earnestly trust that your honorable body will grant our petition the ultimate aim of which is to reduce crime, and to make of our children good citizens.

Signed:

Atlanta, Georgia.   Mrs. L. B. Hope, Chairman
August 19, 1913   in behalf of the Women's Civic and
Social Improvement Committee.[34]

The board discussed possible remedies to the reported conditions: bonds, a special tax, new allocations from existing city funds. All met with varying degrees of disapproval. Board member James L. Key reacted by stating that he believed the conditions had been exaggerated and that "this agitation is going to do the schools more harm than good." He had formerly made it known to the committee members that teachers—"the girls"—were not compelled to teach double sessions but wanted to, and he thought "it better to have poor schools than have the children out of school."[35]

The clerk of the council reported that the city had authorized the purchase of a lot in East Atlanta on which to build a modern school to relieve congestion at the Inman Park, Faith, East Atlanta, and Grant Park (all white) schools. In this connection the council had also "authorized the expenditures of $5,000 of bond money left over from the Fourth Ward Negro School fund to be applied to the erection of a building on the lot donated to the city by Clark University for a Negro School in South Atlanta."[36]

The board reacted by appointing a special committee to make recommendations. By November this committee recommended to the City Council and the Board of Education that the literary course in Black schools end with the sixth grade and that the course of study of the six grades include industrial work and be redistributed over a period of eight years. The members of the Social Improvement Committee objected to the "type of education suggested" and saw such actions as "fundamentally undemocratic and unjust." They pointed out that currently Black children had to be transferred from one school to another in order to enter the seventh and eighth grades. This situation could be corrected by building more schools for Blacks. They opposed limiting the literary course for Black children to six grades while allowing white children a literary course for eight grades and a high school at the public's expense. "To open opportunities for industrial courses is a step . . . desired; but it is to be hoped that the facilities for seventh and eighth grade work will in no way be curtailed . . . for the Negro youth. In this matter, we are sure that we express the sentiments of the great majority of Negro citizens. . . . The public schools are supported by the taxes of all people and to confine the Negro population to a peculiar type of education against its will" would mean open discrimination.[37]

The immediate results were unsettling for the women's committee. A small school was built in South Atlanta on a lot donated by Clark, and the Black teachers' salaries were raised, but the board failed to address other major concerns uncovered by the women. Black schools still suffered extreme overcrowding, double sessions (triple sessions after 1923), inadequate and unsafe recreational facilities, and extreme understaffing. The union continued its efforts through 1914 and 1915. After such men as John Hope, the Reverend Peter James Bryant, and the Reverend A. D. Williams (grandfather of Martin Luther King, Jr.) joined the campaign, the union was able to acquire some improvements for Black schools and to express its dissatisfactions more effectively: two attempts by the board to float bonds for school construction were defeated by Blacks because appropriations were not made for Black schools.

In 1921 the city proposed another bond issue, this time for $4 million, for the construction of schools. This time the union worked with other citizens to get the bonds issued, because the board had finally promised that $1,250,000 of the sum would go for improvements in the Black schools. The union worked zealously to get Blacks out to the polls, for one-third of the white voting public opposed the bonds. Mass meetings were held throughout the city. Black and white poll-watchers kept vigil to ensure fraud-free elections.[38]

Superintendent of Schools William Slaton, in order to soften the issue, had for several years granted the union's requests to use Black schools for civic purposes. Beginning in 1910, Slaton allowed the Roach Street school to be used as a neighborhood center, the first time such a use was permitted. By 1912 the Roach, Storrs, and Pittsburg schools were used for summer vacation schools, for public meetings, and for extra classes—kindergarten, Bible study, health, basketry, folk dancing, dressmaking, cooking, and needlework. Each class had three instructors who volunteered many hours of services. In 1912 the union's lecture series presented Booker T. Washington and raised more than three hundred dollars. These funds were used to purchase a permanent settlement house, where even more educational opportunities could be offered. The following summer Slaton increased the number of schools used in the extracurricular program, and the Presbyterian Mission conducted daily vacation Bible school classes at several local churches to assist the union.[39]

Though the women's committee did not solve the complex problems of inadequate school facilities for Black children in Atlanta, this was the first organized effort to investigate and confront the blatant racism of the City Council and the Board of Education. The union kept up its challenge of segregation in the public school system in Atlanta, and these efforts eventually contributed to the opening of Atlanta's first Black high school, Booker T. Washington, in 1924.

In June 1914, as a result of the findings of the Women's Social and Civic Improvement Committee, the Atlanta Anti-Tuberculosis Association took the initiative in calling a meeting, inviting representatives from various Black organizations to meet in order "for the white and Negro people to unite in their efforts for public health in Atlanta." Representatives of Atlanta's Black insurance agencies, the YMCA, the ministerial alliances, the medical society, the public school system, the nursing service, the college communities, and other civic and social groups met with the Anti-Tuberculosis Association to coordinate and unite the work under way to promote public health in all of Atlanta's communities.[40]

The discussion that ensued revealed that in all of the Black organizations there was a social service department (under a variety of names) and that social welfare work was ongoing. Two anti-tuberculosis leagues were already in existence in the Black Third and Fourth wards. Since 1907, when tuberculosis clinics opened in Atlanta, Black patients had been receiving aid. In 1909 a "colored clinic" was opened with white nurses and doctors and with an educational campaign conducted by Black volunteers in Black churches and schools. What was now needed was a citywide coordination of the existing services. It was suggested that new surveys be conducted in the city's Black sections and a general committee set up with members from a variety of organizations, including the union (with Lugenia as its representative), to survey the public health conditions in the schools. Another committee was organized to survey the sanitary conditions in the homes. Concern extended far beyond tuberculosis. Plans were made for doctors and nurses to conduct lectures. The medical society initiated a special training program for nurses who then would be hired in maternal and child health care centers operated by churches and civic groups. The society also suggested that a Black health officer be hired for Atlanta's Black sections.

Ferdinand Burns, Lugenia's father (left);
Lugenia's mother, Louisa M. Bertha Burns,
her brother Adolph, and Lugenia (below)
(Emma and Lloyd Lewis Papers,
The University Library, University of Illinois
at Chicago)

Lugenia and son John Hope II
(Emma and Lloyd Lewis Papers,
The University Library, University of Illinois
at Chicago)

John, John II, Edward, and Lugenia Hope on the porch of the president's house, Morehouse College, about 1916 (Emma and Lloyd Lewis Papers, The University Library, University of Illinois at Chicago)

Lugenia Burns Hope, about 1912
(Special Collections and Archives, Atlanta
University Center, Robert Woodruff Library)

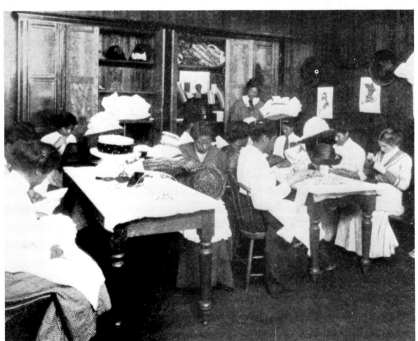

Lugenia (standing, rear) teaching a millinery class at Spelman College
in 1913
(From Joseph R. Gay, *Self-Educator for a Rising Race: A Practical Manual
of Ambitious Colored Americans* [Nashville, 1913])

Lugenia (front row, second from the right) and members of the Atlanta YWCA. The members of the Black branch of the Atlanta YWCA were successful in opening the Phillis Wheatley branch after much conflict and tension from regional headquarters.
(Special Collections and Archives, Atlanta University Center, Robert Woodruff Library)

Lugenia (center) and members of the Neighborhood Union. The Neighborhood Union was the first female agency in the city to address the educational, medical, social, and recreational needs of Black Atlantans. Its structure and agenda for community building became a role model for such work on both national and international levels.
(Special Collections and Archives, Atlanta University Center, Robert Woodruff Library)

Lugenia Burns Hope, about 1940
(Emma and Lloyd Lewis Papers,
The University Library, University of Illinois
at Chicago)

Lugenia (back row, right) and members of the International Council of Women of the Darker Races. ICWDR, organized by southern Black women, emerged during the Pan-African consciousness following World War I. The organization brought together women of color in examining global issues of race, gender, class, and peace.
(Special Collections and Archives, Atlanta University Center, Robert Woodruff Library)

The meeting adopted the Neighborhood Union's plan of organization, dividing the city into sixteen zones, using volunteer workers, and having districts, district directors, and zone chairpersons. Their motto for the municipal cleanup campaign was "Burn, Bury and Beautify." A Black branch of the Anti-Tuberculosis Association was instituted in 1915, with John Hope as chairman, Henry H. Pace as president, and Rosa Lowe as secretary. By 1916 a Black nurse had been employed as a member of the association's nursing staff. That year 143 workers visited 5,406 homes and reached 23,771 occupants; an additional 16,526 Atlantans were contacted by special workers.[41]

The spring of 1917 witnessed a great Medico-Educational Campaign in cooperation with the Negro Clean-Up Week, a contest sponsored by the National Negro Business League. One mass meeting numbered over 1,300 people, and 54 speakers addressed people in 27 churches and Sunday schools. Workers visited 3,786 homes and reached 13,000 occupants. Fifteen portable free clinics were opened every day for fourteen weeks in different parts of the city, giving medical assistance to 641 people. Beginning in 1915 and running through 1917, classes offering lectures on health and sanitation were established in the public schools. These lectures, sponsored by the association, were also given in each of the eight public Black schools. As a result of this campaign, Atlanta was awarded the National Silver Cup by the National Negro Business League.[42]

The work of the association in connection with the clean-up campaign of the Business League continued despite the distractions of World War I; in fact, the work was more systematically organized, obtaining better results. Clean-up campaigns not only attacked the dirty premises of white merchants in Black areas but also specifically assailed the merchants' fraudulent sales practices, such as substituting rocks for some of the flour in a bag to increase its weight. In addition, they reprimanded store owners for not covering garbage containers or screening the windows to keep germ-carrying flies from infesting the food.[43]

In June 1919 Lugenia became the full-time "colored" educational agent for the association. Under her direction the Black branch began to attain financial solvency through solicitation of needed funds. Previously a monthly sum of sixty dollars had been raised for the educational agent for Blacks, when such a worker could be secured. Lugenia worked without salary and then, after setting up the department, relinquished her work to a Spelman graduate, Carrie Dukes, who became the first paid Black worker in the association's office. She was succeeded by Katherine Kelley, who was the last paid Black visiting health educator. Following her untimely death, the association chose a white woman to be director of the colored educational work, and this practice was continued subsequently.[44]

The clean-up campaigns and the Black anti-tuberculosis efforts were ongoing and won various second-place and honorable mention awards from the National Negro Business League's annual Silver Cup presentations. In 1924 one Black home in Atlanta was the federal government's model home, used in promoting its National Better Homes Week contest.

Realizing the necessity of "enlightening the neighborhood workers along the lines of health and sanitation," and the need "to help and encourage these community workers to do a better piece of work in their respective neighborhoods," Lugenia organized a Social Service Institute at Morehouse in September of 1919. The theme was, "Make the world safe for babies and children." Lugenia believed that the way to reach this goal was to "banish ignorance by educating people on health and social problems. Race marches forth on feet of little children but feet of little children do get such poor starts sometimes."[45]

The institute decided to limit its membership to zone chairmen, lieutenants, and the leading social workers of the churches. Participants were expected to carry useful information back to their respective communities. Though the planned enrollment was fifty, ninety-seven people signed up, so that double sessions were necessary. Classes included home nursing, the prevention and cure of tuberculosis, oral hygiene for mothers and infants, proper detection and care of "feeblemindedness" in children, child nutrition, proper treatment of the eyes, and the methods of social work. Institute faculty consisted of Professor Gary Moore, the director; Mary Dickerson and Rosa Lowe of the Anti-Tuberculosis Association; Ludie Andrews, a registered nurse; Lawrence Reddick, a historian; and several others.

In the fall of 1920 the National Conference of Social Workers discussed the need for a school of social work for Blacks. One of Atlanta's delegates, Robert Dexter, director of the Associated Charities, brought the message back to Atlanta and called together some of its leading citizens: Jesse Thomas, director of the Atlanta branch of the Urban League; John Hope; Myron Adams of Atlanta University; Lugenia Hope; and Plato Durham of Emory University. Out of this meeting emerged the Atlanta School of Social Service, housed at Morehouse, with Moore as its director. The announcement stated that the objective was to "afford an opportunity for training in the principles and techniques of social work to colored young men and women." Special concentration would be on training Black leadership. It was believed that Atlanta offered the best opportunity of any southern city for the creation of such a school, for it possessed a large black population, an improved climate of race relations, and several schools of higher learning. In addition, Atlanta had several leading organizations with "strong colored" departments, and it was the southern headquarters of the Urban League.[46]

The plan was to offer a one-year course in social theory and practice to qualified students, commencing in September 1920 and continuing through the academic year. The course of study included economic and social theory, medical-social problems, psychology and mental problems, social casework, community organization, statistics and record keeping, and fieldwork. In addition, an evening course of ten public sessions was offered, with guest lecturers addressing the topic "The Field of Social Work." Again the enrollment was limited. Applicants were expected to be at least twenty years of age, with a high school diploma or its equivalent. Tuition was twenty-five dollars annually. Certificates would be awarded to students who satisfactorily completed the year's work. A graduate could then qualify for any of a number of positions: district agent or executive in the Colored Department of the Associated Charities or a similar organization, probation officer in the juvenile courts, recreational director, attendance officer, Urban League secretary or assistant, welfare worker in industry, assistant in the social services department of a church, YWCA, or YMCA. The need for qualified personnel was so great as nearly to guarantee placement for those who earned certificates; in fact, the course pamphlet carried a warning that the faculty reserved the right to ask any student who "showed definite unfitness for social work" to withdraw from the school.[47]

The faculty consisted of many of the instructors of Lugenia's 1919 institute, along with Marion C. Pruitt (Atlanta School of Medicine), Newdigate M. Ownesby (Baltimore University), Robert C. Dexter (Atlanta Associated Charities), and Lugenia herself. Salaries were subsidized by the agencies furnishing the faculty.[48] Morehouse assumed responsibility for housing the school and for furnishing some of its personnel until the school became a separate, self-supporting professional school, incorporated in 1925 as the Atlanta School of Social Work.

After becoming independent, the school relocated to Auburn Avenue in the Herndon Building, also the home of the Atlanta Urban League. In 1927 Forrester B. Washington became its director. Six years later the school moved to the Atlanta University campus. Talks of affiliation and consolidation began during John Hope's tenure. After much deliberation, trustees of the university authorized the Atlanta School of Social Work to become a member of the Atlanta University System as of September 1, 1938, at which time it became officially known as the Atlanta University School of Social Work.[49]

By 1920 the work of the Neighborhood Union had received national recognition. Because of the organization's assistance to the Red Cross during the Atlanta fire of 1917, the union was presented with a commendation from the national chairman of the Red Cross, Calvin Coolidge. When Mississippi was struck with the great flood of 1927, the federal government appropriated over $5 million for Red Cross aid and Secretary of Commerce Herbert Hoover asked Lugenia to assist the Red Cross's relief project in Mississippi. Along with Robert R. Moton of Tuskegee and L. McCoy of Nashville, she became a member of the Colored Advisory Committee, sent to investigate the care of the "colored population refugee camps, to receive suggestions and complaints and make necessary investigation so as to give complete assurance of proper handling of this question."[50]

The commission members arrived at the camps in June 1927. Before they got there they had received complaints of neglect and discrimination from Black victims. The complainants wanted the commission to inspect the housing at Black camps, the health conditions, the lack of food and cots, and the general discrimination Black refugees faced at the hands of white officials. As the commission members started their investigation, they noted the forced labor required of Black male refugees in the construction of levees. They were informed that Black male refugees were not allowed to leave the camps to return to their farms and homes, even if they were in a position to return, unless a white person had written a certificate of support. If the Black male refused to work, then his family would not receive rations unless, again, he had a certificate of support from a white person. To avoid this indignity, Black women came to get their supplies with certificates from whites declaring them widows. This practice continued until the Red Cross ruled that women and children with no man in the family would no longer be eligible for rations.[51]

The commission began its investigation of Mississippi in all-Black Mound Bayou, Cohoma County, Vicksburg, and Matchen. For the most part, except in those camps with sick refugees, the commission found health and sanitary conditions acceptable. However, no "special precautions were taken in any of the camps visited to prevent the spread of venereal diseases among the refugees." There were other problems of a more immediate nature as well. Some landowners charged their tenants for the supplies furnished by the Red Cross. In some camps every person was required to have a pass, and there were cases where Blacks with passes were roughly handled and insulted. The Black community opposed the presence of the National Guard, which was stationed in many of the camps, because Blacks suffered discrimination and physical abuse from the troops. In the Vicksburg camp a group of twenty-five male refugees, corralled after an attempt to leave the camp to avoid forced work, were severely whipped by the guardsmen.[52] The commission noted that the best-run camps were those in which the Black residents had a voice, such as in Greensville. Recommendations for alleviating neglect, abuse, and discrimination constituted the final report of the Colored Advisory Commission. The report was received with much fanfare, and the commission's bulletin was published, yet few of the recommendations were instituted.

At home in Atlanta, the union continued its community programs. By 1930 these were confined to health work among preschool children, but in 1931 citizens begged the union to examine the unemployment in the Black communities and to help in relieving the suffering caused by the depression. An Emergency Commission of seventy-five women and teachers from the schools of the Atlanta University System visited every family of the West Side to find the needy and to solicit aid. District groups were asked to aid the unemployed in their respective regions. The committee hosted street carnivals to raise funds and to help "keep the unemployed in good cheer which at a time like this is necessary." These efforts raised $600. "With this money . . . and the regular contribution of groceries and clothing [between March 1931 and April 1932] we were able to help 1189 families. Groceries amounting to $300.00, 1890 garment[s] and 13 tons coal were despersed [*sic*]."[53]

In July 1933 the union celebrated its twenty-fifth anniversary. The celebration began with a pageant that dramatically portrayed the organization's history, growth, and accomplishments; the highlight was the blending of symbolic dances with a reenactment and interpretation of various phases of the union. Children who had formerly been patients of the health clinics presented a play; exhibits were displayed; and the union held a mass meeting.

The culminating event of the celebration was a testimonial banquet for Lugenia to honor her twenty-five years of social service to Atlanta. An assortment of social, religious, and educational leaders reflected on her as a "civic leader," a "friend of the public," a "national character," and the "founder of the Neighborhood Union." The Atlanta community showered her with gifts of appreciation. Recollections and testimonies noted her unselfish service to the city and the country as a whole. She was honored for her "power of leadership," her "fearless stand for justice," her efforts to "interpret black needs and desires to white America," and her agitation for "equal opportunities for black girls, particularly in the South." Mary McLeod Bethune spoke of Lugenia's methods of challenging injustice, recalling how Lugenia often became impatient at tactics that prevented or hampered progress in race relations. Though there were occasions when Lugenia's vocal agitations were not appreciated, Bethune went on, no one ever questioned her integrity or her fairness; and her capacity to get results proved the effectiveness of her approach.[54]

On July 8, 1935, after twenty-seven years of founding, developing, and nurturing the growth and progress of her idea for the Neighborhood Union, Lugenia Burns Hope submitted her letter of resignation as an officer and member. Lugenia, then sixty-four, had tried before to resign, but the board had always refused her resignation. At this July meeting, however, John was present. He told the board that his wife wanted to resign because her duties were very heavy (he did not elaborate on what duties), and he believed that it was time for a change in administration as the organization continued to grow. The board members could not ignore this appeal; they accepted the resignation.[55]

Under Lugenia's leadership, the efforts of this group of educated, middle-class, Black women in Atlanta had run the gamut from services and programs to issues and protests. The variety of these offerings alone was a tribute to the organization: a campaign to hire "colored" policemen; a drive to register voters and to get them to pay their poll taxes; a Pre-Census Educational Campaign to inform the community of the role of the census; a program for French war orphans during World War I, for which Lugenia received a medal from the French government; a free Easter egg hunt, the only such event for Black children in the city; a petition to improve the city's facilities in Washington's Park, the only Black public park; a petition for better police protection in Black communities; temperance campaigns; affiliation with the National Association of Colored Women in 1914, for which the union established the neighborhood and citizenship departments, with Lugenia serving as the chairperson for both; a campaign to get a truant officer, a physical education director, and free kindergartens instituted in the public schools; improvement in railroad accommodations; better streetcar schedules; homes for wayward girls; the protection of Black women and girls living in rural districts; a petition to the state to improve the sanitariums and expand the hiring of Black nurses; and many others. The union's energies and concerns seem to have had no limitations.

The women of the Neighborhood Union saw their organization as an experiment in community cooperation, designed "to build the sort of ethnic pride that would take delight in constructive citizenship and happy family life."[56] The founders and leadership core of the union were mostly middle-class, educated women, many the wives of faculty members in surrounding colleges or of prominent Black Atlantans. Their privileged positions gave them high visibility and enabled them to gain audiences with the city's power structure, to which they could present the problems and needs of Black Atlanta in an organized, structured, and articulate manner. They emerged as the most vocal arm of the Black community in petitioning against and protesting the segregation and discrimination faced by Black Atlantans. They waged relentless campaigns to have essential services provided in their communities: medical and dental care, recreational facilities, improved schools, better sanitation, and safer streets.

These women were not only educated and middle-class; they were very much a product of their times: Victorian in beliefs and values. They believed that the uplift of the race was intrinsically bound to "moral uplift," that as women and mothers they were morally superior, and that the "hand that rocks the cradle rules the world." Generally, members of the community respected and trusted these women because of their social prominence, and this attitude usually carried over to the organization. Yet as the union focused on the moral cleansing of communities by means of its Investigation Committee, it is not clear from either the oral or the written records how all of the neighborhood folks reacted. The union's drives to close saloons, dives, and houses of prostitution, which were viewed as contributing factors in the moral corruption of young girls and boys, centered only on removing these vices from the members' immediate neighborhoods. In most cases the activity merely moved across the street or across town—into another Black community. Value judgments of the union's leadership hindered permanent efforts to assist or "save" the "fallen." Because union members believed that poverty and the lack of proper instruction and supervision were factors that led young people to pursue lives of crime, they concentrated on "capturing" young adults before they became victims of vice. Thus they saw it as their mission to provide the young with alternatives and the parents with information.

Though many of the union's projects were successful, many others, of course, met with failure: few unpaved streets were paved by the municipal government; streetlights were secured in some instances only after a fatal accident; police protection in Black communities remained negligible; and the City Council turned a deaf ear to the union's fight to secure the hiring of Black policemen to patrol their communities. Still, the union was the strongest and most visible community-controlled agency for Blacks in Atlanta. And it did enjoy substantial successes. Led by an aggressive, conscientious, and totally committed founder, the union emerged as a national and international role model for community organization. The spirit and philosophy of its founding members can be summed up in the following lines, chosen as the organization's motto:

> But I turned not away from their smiles nor their tears—
> Both parts of an infinite plan;—
> Let me live in my house by the side of the road
> And be a friend to man.[57]

Chapter Five

Toward Racial Uplift

Before the initiation of an interracial movement in the South and the decision to include women in that male-dominated movement, southern Black women, individually and collectively, had organized programs to "uplift" the quality of Black life. Either through their local community agencies or through regional, national, and international activism, they were in the foreground of progressive reform. They provided the needed leadership and emerged as leaders in both the southern and the national Black women's movements.

Because of their recognized leadership, when the interracial movement began in the South, many of these women—along with their husbands—were the first to be asked to join. As the women's division developed in such organizations as the Commission on Interracial Cooperation, Black women found that there were some southern white women who wanted to improve race relations and who were eager to join them in their campaigns.[1] Though there were examples of success in these endeavors, Black women found that in most cases southern white women could not completely divorce themselves from their belief in segregation and racial inferiority, and they were thus not completely willing to accept their Black colleagues as peers. A case in point is the development of the Black branches of the YWCA in the South.

At the time of the organization of the YWCA in the South (1906), there were no Black branches. There were, however, a few groups organized by the association among Black female students at government and foundation schools, such as the one introduced at Spelman College in 1884. Any decision the National Board might make in regard to these student groups therefore inevitably involved the overall policy of the YWCA in work among Blacks.

In June 1907 a special conference was held in Asheville, North Carolina, to consider the matter of YWCA work in the southern Black communities. Sixty southern white women attended. The student report from the South was presented, whereupon it was decided that Black student groups should be allowed to continue their affiliation with the national movement. Southern city associations were not required to work in the Black community; in fact, no mention was even made of this possibility. The paramount concern here was the possibility of Blacks' attending national conventions and conferences, an alarming probability if Blacks became members, since these events were open to all delegates. To deter this potential embarrassment, the conference resolved that there would be but one association in the community: "If other Association groups existed in a city . . . they were to be in a 'Branch' relationship." Nowhere was it specifically written that the YWCA would be white, "but this was apparently taken for granted." Branches could be organized in any city where the number of Blacks seemed "to warrant it." But it was made clear that these branches were to be under the direct supervision of the Department of Method of the National Board, and they were not to be "related to the 'central' city association in their community."[2]

This policy contributed to an increase in the number of Black branches in the North and the organization of Black branches in the South. Black delegates attended the national convention in

1913, which convened in Richmond, Virginia, and were assigned segregated seating in the balcony. It was only in the student associations that Black delegates from the South were permitted to participate in intercollegiate activities as regular members.[3]

In order to facilitate and coordinate this new growth, the YWCA established a biracial Sub-Committee for Colored Work in 1913. Eva Bowles, appointed the first secretary for "colored work," was assigned to work with city associations. Minutes from the first committee meeting described its establishment as "frankly experimental," declaring: "Now we shall be able to develop the work. There has been much discussion of it in the past, often as an excuse for doing nothing. We believe that things may be actually done and handled effectively, if we are able to deal more intelligently with the problems through mutual understanding and sympathies."[4] This committee, organized out of New York with little input from southern white or Black women, met regularly but did not formulate any official policy or take any particular action. Instead, it planned the YWCA's second special conference, held in Louisville, Kentucky, in October 1915 in order to continue the organization of Black YWCA work.

Unlike the Asheville meeting, the Louisville conference saw a large number of Black branches represented by their own leaders. Blacks representing various other organizations also attended, with the intention of gaining information on how to establish Black YWCA branches in their respective communities. Lugenia was a delegate from Atlanta. A Committee on Findings, recognizing the "absolute need of mutual understanding and patience on the part of both . . . white and colored women from or of the South," announced that the time had come to appoint a biracial committee of southern women. The Committee on Findings recommended (1) training young Black women for leadership positions; (2) establishing student conferences for inspiration and for developing student leadership; (3) cooperating in city associations through branch relationships; (4) developing a plan for implementing colored work; and (5) inviting white secretaries or leaders to visit Black schools, colleges, and conferences. The committee further advised that YWCA secretaries should be intelligent, full of Christian spirit, patient, appreciative of the group with whom they would work, and possessed of administrative ability.[5]

As a result of this committee's report, the National Board concluded that Black delegates at the Louisville conference would endorse a limited development of YWCA work for Black women in the South, a policy by which this work would progress only as fast as the white women of each community permitted. But after the policy was proposed to the convention and passed, the southern Black women rose in protest: they wanted autonomy over their branches and representation on all supervisory boards and committees.

The ensuing fight to bring parity in the YWCA was temporarily halted by the beginning of World War I and the YWCA's war work. At the outbreak of the war the YWCA developed the National War Work Council. With a budget of $1 million, the council provided community centers, "approved" shelters for women working in industrial factories, and hostess houses provided recreational activities and served as places for soldiers to visit with family members and friends. The council also received requests to help with emergency housing for Black workers and to establish hostess houses near the cantonments where Black troops were in training. To raise funds Patriotic Service Leagues, offering classes in food demonstration, table service, tennis, and stenography, were set up in various cities. One year before the Armistice, the YWCA appropriated $200,000 for a colored department of the War Work Council. Eva Bowles was placed in charge, with a small staff to assist her. By the end of 1919, Bowles and her staff had established recreational and industrial centers in forty-five communities. Paid Black local workers rose from nine in 1915 to eighty-six, and the total number of Black women enrolled in branches grew to twelve thousand.[6]

In Atlanta the Neighborhood Union formed the core of the city's Colored Women's War Council. The union, under Lugenia's supervision, applied its organizational structure—the division of the city into zones and of zones into neighborhoods—in planning council work in the city. Volunteers were assigned in each of the neighborhood units. Four patriotic clinics with a membership of two hundred were organized by Agnes D. Jones, secretary of the Patriotic League Drive. Eighteen homes were opened to out-of-town relatives of the soldiers at Camp Gordon; while the maximum rate for board and lodging was set at one hundred dollars per family, some Atlantans were willing to accommodate needy families for several days for free. Following an extensive survey of the city, the council recommended that (1) provost guards stationed in Black sections of Atlanta be chosen with great care and be reliable and dependable in character; (2) Black soldiers be protected on streetcars; (3) there be an end to mistreatment of Black people—civilians and soldiers—by police officers of both city and county; (4) there be accessibility to all public parks and places of recreation for all soldiers; (5) there be proper lighting in facilities for Black soldiers; (6) sanitary and Prohibition laws be enforced; and (7) vice be suppressed. The council succeeded in raising eighteen hundred dollars to aid in building the YWCA center for recreational use by Black soldiers and their families at Camp Gordon.[7]

On the basis of her outstanding work with the Atlanta council, Lugenia was appointed Special War Work Secretary and placed in charge of training hostess-house workers at Camp Upton, New York. As early as November 1917 the YWCA had received requests to establish a hostess house at Camp Upton. The federal government donated a facility. The YWCA then decided that since there would "always be a certain number of colored troops at Camp Upton," a building should be erected for use as a Black hostess house. Because of its nearness to the national headquarters, Bowles suggested, it would be appropriate to use this house as the model for hostess-house training. The house was opened on these principles in early 1918. Three volunteers were placed in charge of the workers, but as the work increased it became necessary to hire someone permanent, and Lugenia was asked to "take charge" of the program. For a salary of a hundred dollars per month, a possible month's vacation, and a monthly board and room fee of forty dollars, she came to Camp Upton. For over five months she provided instructions to workers in training and gave assistance to the soldiers, many of whom told her that they "would have deserted long ago had it not been for this place." Reflecting on the house and her part, she stated: "So much devolves upon women to maintain and promote real civilization in the midst of this present orgy of death and destruction and I am most thankful that I could spend at least a few months from my own sons to cheer, direct and comfort thousands of sons of other mothers."[8]

Following World War I, the Colored Women's War Council was dismantled and the Committee on Colored Work was reorganized to function on a wider basis. Now the Bureau of Colored Work, it held its first meeting in February 1920 and began to work toward establishing the standards for Black branches.

Once back in Atlanta, Lugenia tried to form a Black branch there. Susan L. Davis, president of the central YWCA in the city, was very supportive and encouraged the plan. Opposition came from Adella Ruffin, the field supervisor of colored work in the South, who was headquartered in Richmond. The Atlanta women, through their field secretary, Beatrice Walker, extended an invitation to Ruffin to address their group and to learn of their efforts to establish a Black branch. Walker organized the girls in the public schools and the churches, but she was handicapped by not having a community center. A suitable house was located; Ruffin, however, though she did make several trips to Atlanta, never gave permission to secure the facility. In addition, the hoped-for relationship between the Black group and the central association of the city failed to develop. The National Board required that before a branch could be launched the branch relationship had to be established. Accordingly, a committee of three white women and two Black women was asked to link the branch with the central association and to serve as an advisory committee. The three white women were selected, but the two Black women were never appointed by the South Atlantic Office.

At this point a Miss Kennedy was sent to replace Walker, but not allowed to purchase a center or to establish an advisory committee. Ruffin instructed the new secretary to consult on these matters with the hostess-house director at Camp Gordon. The women of Atlanta were upset: the director was an "absolute stranger to Atlanta and knew nothing of the people and the conditions." Even so, she called a meeting of the Black women of the city to assist her. Three people attended, Lugenia among them. Lugenia insisted that these three people could not possibly assume the responsibility for selecting a center. She suggested that a larger group be assembled, and a larger committee was indeed organized to investigate possible locations. This group recommended two locations, one on Edgewood Avenue and one on Piedmont Avenue. Though the Piedmont Avenue house was a better building, the Edgewood Avenue house was located in a better neighborhood. Yet Ruffin settled on the Piedmont Avenue house, signed a lease on this property, and immediately dismissed the local field secretary—all without assembling or informing the local committee or the field secretary herself. The Atlanta women were convinced that the Piedmont house was not a suitable place for working with girls and that the difficulties of immediately purging that locality of its "lewd and disorderly" people made it an impracticable choice.[9]

Ruffin's response to the women who questioned her actions was arrogant. As Lugenia put it:

> She wanted us to understand that we could get nothing without going by her, that she was no novice in organizations. . . . She had transacted the business for the house, and they [Black women] were going into that house and if we did not want to abide by that decision she would leave Atlanta and come at some other time and she would say that Atlanta was not ready for the work.[10]

Some of the women in Atlanta still thought it was worth another effort to work with Ruffin. Others, Lugenia included, raised objections to Ruffin's leadership. But Ruffin had gained the support of the white field staff in Richmond and was determined "to use their authority to bolster her position" and to prevent the Black secretaries of the National Board from coming South.[11]

Growing increasingly determined to integrate Black women into the YWCA on a basis of full equality, Black southern women sought to clarify the principles on which work in the Black community should be based. These women had been very active with the War Work Council, and after the war their aim was to make the YWCA more sensitive to local needs. In particular, they were outraged at the YWCA's assumption that they were incapable of choosing their own leaders and that their branch work could therefore progress only as fast as southern white women would permit. The YWCA, in rebuttal, maintained that this approach had been decided as policy at the Louisville conference and endorsed by the Black delegates in attendance.

Lugenia, one of the Black delegates at Louisville, called a meeting in April 1920 in her home to clarify the results of the Louisville meeting and to organize a protest. "Northern women," she explained, "thought they knew more about it than Southern women. Colored women believed they know more than both and that's why they wanted to represent themselves." The Blacks asserted adamantly that the Louisville policy was a gross misrepresentation of their position on the development of YWCA work among Blacks in the South. Louisville delegates Charlotte Hawkins Brown, Nettie L. Napier (represented by a Mrs. Hall), and Lugenia strongly maintained that the Louisville conference had been called to "talk over plans but not to decide anything." They insisted that the understanding had been that the first YWCA organized in a city would be an "Interlocking Committee" composed of members from both the Black branch and the white association, with a larger number from the branch. "There was nothing said of the work in this field not advancing any faster than the Southern whites will permit, as has lately been affirmed."[12]

These women were also opposed to having southern white women dictate the policy on Black collegiate work. Lugenia thought that all student work ought to be directed from the Bureau of Colored Work in New York. As she expressed the issue to the director of the bureau: "First because of barriers which have been built up by her own race, she [the southern white woman] has never put herself in a position to know colored people, and knows absolutely nothing of our student life in the colored schools and colleges of the Southland."[13] Nonetheless, in 1920 southern whites launched a campaign to replace Catherine D. Lealtad, the Black national student secretary, with a southern white woman who, according to National Headquarters, was "really sincere and just in her attitude toward colored people." Receiving little support for her stand on equal accommodations for Black staff members at national conventions, and refusing to work under a southern white woman, Lealtad became disgusted with the whole matter and resigned to join the Urban League.[14] Lugenia and her fellow Black Louisville delegates saw an unjust precedent in situations like this one. They feared that Black people would not accept white southern control and that the overall effect would be unfavorable to the work of the YWCA.

These Black women also protested a statement of Ruffin's concerning the type of girls the YWCA should serve, a statement that had caused much unrest. Ruffin accused Lugenia of attempting to use the organization to "save immoral Alley Girls," instead of helping aspiring middle-class women. The Black women agreed that the YWCA was not an organization for rescue work but asserted that "a good girl [living] in the 'alley' should not be cut off from the opportunities offered by the YWCA."[15]

A committee consisting of Mary Jackson McCrorey, Charlotte Hawkins Brown, Marion B. Wilkerson, Frances Keyser, and Lugenia was charged with drawing up an appeal. Lucy Laney, Mary J. McCrorey, and Lugenia were chosen to present the document to Eva Bowles and Mary Cratty at the national headquarters and at the next national conference, scheduled for Cleveland, Ohio. The caucus of Black southern women who signed the petition declared that through their professional and organizational affiliations they represented over three hundred thousand Black women of the South. In addition to requesting the removal of Ruffin, this caucus sought to discover the cause of the general dissatisfaction and unrest among the "Black women of the South who are interested in associated work." These women's desires to become more involved were constantly frustrated. The petitioners questioned why the national office of the YWCA permitted its field secretaries to ignore local conditions when they entered new fields. They asked why the supervision of colored work could not be directed from the national office. They demanded that "in all work affecting our people full recognition of leadership be given Negro women." They also urged that a Black woman be appointed to represent them on the National Board. By far their most important grievance was that "the Southern white woman does not understand us and therefore we ask that we be permitted to form independent organizations wherever the branch relationship is not desirable or where there is no central association."[16]

The Black southern delegates attending the national conference in Cleveland in May 1920 told the entire convention that they had been misrepresented at the Louisville conference on two counts: (1) the claim that they had agreed to a policy of Jim Crow association and (2) the charge that they had agreed to a policy of discrimination. Addressing the conference, Lugenia stated that the executive of the South Atlantic Field "is given over to the idea that the work cannot go any faster than the white women will permit." Lugenia assured those in attendance that Blacks did not support this interpretation. She threatened that southern Black women "would rather go back to [their] church organizations than have a special policy for colored women under the direction of a Southern white woman who knows absolutely nothing about us." She warned further that "we as Negro women must remember that whatever policy the Southern Colored women stand for is to be the policy by which the whole Negro race of women will be governed. Therefore we must stand and contend for what is to be the policy for the future generations."[17] In fact, Lugenia challenged the National Board to resume the direction of branch work, since the Southern Field Committee did not seem willing to confer with Black women, who should have been members of the policy-making group.

The Cleveland conference concurred that at the Louisville conference no agreement had been reached that Black women would organize only when white women in the area decided they were ready. The Cleveland delegates did not, however, support the Black women's request to establish independent associations. The organization's executives saw the branch relationship as ideal for the betterment of interracial understanding. If Black women in a given area were ready for a branch and the central association was not, the Black members affected should write the National Board, which would send a representative "to see that the work was started." The board took no action on the request for the addition of a Black to its membership. Its members were elected, the board explained; the criteria that applied to white candidates would also apply to Blacks. The request to permit national secretaries to visit the field was discussed. The Black southern delegates were instructed to write to both the field and national headquarters on the question of branch personnel. Claiming that it was not able to review and rule on all regional policies, the board referred to the southern field staff the problems in its jurisdiction; to complete this task, the board suggested a committee meeting in Richmond to resolve regional difficulties.[18]

Disappointed that the National Board did not resolve all the issues her committee had raised, McCrorey concluded that the "whole policy is to keep us strictly subordinated, and that is the price those women must pay for their jobs." She warned that some "of us [Black women] must keep wide awake and remain fearless to stand by the thing we know to be square and helpful to the colored woman . . . without sacrifice of principle."[19]

Immediately after Cleveland, the Black women's caucus began to draw up a definite plan for the Richmond meeting in order to avoid any misunderstanding. Again in Richmond the Black caucus presented its fundamental demands. In trying to settle once and for all the issue of the relationship of branches to the central association, Eva Bowles told the Black delegates—Laney, McCrorey, and Lugenia—that when the National Board had been organized the question of separate development in the North and the South had been raised. Some of the organizers had feared that one section of the country might try to force the other to develop work faster than that section wished or could. An agreement had then apparently been reached that if the National Board was organized for work throughout the country, no section would be urged to develop faster than it felt possible or wise. She explained that whereas colored work had at one time been planned from New York, the National Board had since "recognized that the best method for doing colored work in cities is through [the] branch relationship. . . . [I]t proved not practicable to carry on work from National Board headquarters directly because there could not be direct touch and the work could not succeed without that."[20]

Black caucus members then confronted the national representatives with examples of cities like Jackson, Mississippi, and Little Rock, Arkansas, where Black women's work was blocked because of the attitudes of whites. The national representatives categorically denied the charges, however, declaring again that the branch relationship was the best plan to be followed "under present conditions." To substantiate its position, the board contrasted Atlanta to Little Rock and Jackson. On September 4, 1919, the Black YWCA had opened in Atlanta as the Blue Triangle Center at 128 Piedmont Avenue. (Later the name was changed to the Phillis Wheatley YWCA, and later still, in 1950, the branch moved to its present location at 599 Mitchell Street, Southwest.) The facility served as both a residence and a program center. By 1921 over 350 girls were enrolled in the clubs and classes.[21]

Though the administration of the colored work in the South Atlantic Field was discussed, no mention was made of the caucus's request that Ruffin be fired on the grounds that she did not know the people in her charge. This request was part of a lengthy petition that had been sent to the national headquarters. In response, the board recognized that the "judgement of those colored women living in and interested in a given community might differ from that of the field secretary" and that "certain developments would have been different had the judgement of those . . . interested been always followed." But nonetheless the board made no move to replace Ruffin: southern white women supported her, and Black opposition was essentially overlooked. In sum, the entire meeting proved fruitless. Not only were Black demands rejected; the official account of the meeting forwarded to the National Board ignored them altogether. Furious, McCrorey protested that the report made it appear "that there were no complaints, no issues—*nothing* but an outing to Richmond to see the South Atlantic Field office and its 'dignitaries.'"22

Frustrated by the failure to work from within established channels, the Black women's caucus brought public pressure to bear on the YWCA, securing petitions from the National Association of Colored Women, the Southeastern Federation of Colored Women's Clubs, Black newspapers, and the Black clergy.23 The direct consequence was a second Louisville Conference on Colored Work in February 1921. This meeting was exclusively for the southern personnel and executives from the national headquarters. Vague recommendations supporting student work came out of the meeting, and provisions for training in secretarial leadership in the field of colored work were suggested. But there was no discussion of the methodology or timetable for the implementation of these ideas. Of special interest to the Black women's caucus were three of the recommendations:

> We recommend that all work for colored groups shall [as] soon as practicable be administered through the regular channels of the association, . . . and that each Field Committee shall have a Sub-Committee on Colored Work composed of white and colored women.

> We recommend that the Committee of Management of Local Associations shall be representative of the different groups and interests of the community.

> We further recommend that local Associations be urged to organize and develop the Committee on Colored Work and that the standardizing of this committee be completed as soon as possible.

The one definitive position taken at the 1921 Louisville Conference was the appointment of Charlotte Hawkins Brown to a figurehead post as member-at-large of the southern field staff. This victory had little substance, for the southern field staff appropriated no travel funds to bring the "non-resident" member to Richmond, nor was she always informed of scheduled meetings or encouraged to attend.[24]

Though disappointed and disgusted at the association's vagueness and failure to address their demands directly, the Black women issued a careful response. In keeping with their principle of self-determination and self-expression, they again petitioned for representation on local committees and the National Board. They wanted it clear that they were not opposing the supervision of their work by field committees, but they did seriously oppose the arbitrary assumption of this work by field committees who had made no provisions for Black members or officials. The Black women cited Article Three of the ByLaws for Colored Work, which mandated such representation. They chastised the Louisville recommendations for not being more explicit; for example, who would determine when it was practicable to organize a Black committee? The recommendations did not guarantee that there would be Black membership on the field committees. For the caucus these principles had to be safeguarded in firm guidelines.

The Black women became more persistent in their demands to form independent organizations whenever the branch relationship was not welcomed by the central association in a community, or if such an association was nonexistent. It was totally unfair, they pointed out, to dismiss this matter by referring to the historical fact of segregation and insisting "that the YWCA never in any place nor in any part of its work can go any faster than the people of a community will permit." What that policy amounted to was that the Black women of a community "can not have an Association except as a branch of the white Association and that they must be governed by the will of the white women in initiating such an organization."[25]

In 1922 the National Board, with advice from experts, decided that the best method for handling colored work was, after all, from the national office rather than through branches and central associations. Lugenia wrote Bowles to express her approval for a policy she and her colleagues had worked for over many years. She did not doubt, she noted, that the day would come when the work could be done otherwise, but for the moment, centralized work was appropriate. If the "supervision of Colored work has been centralized . . . and directed by some one who knows and sympathizes with the Colored girl, a very great step has been taken toward a better understanding. I regret that the southern white women have not been taught to think just GIRLS and as long as they can not . . . they can not think clearly for the highest development of the Colored girl." She requested that Ruffin be transferred to some other part of the country in order that the southern work might begin anew. Acknowledging publicly for the first time the amount of hostility she had herself endured for her position, Lugenia confirmed to Bowles:

> I am just as much interested as ever in YWCA work for our Colored girls and women and if you should not find me working in the cause it would be either because some people would not permit me or I could not accept some obviously unchristian and retarding ways of doing things. My heart is in the right place, my health is perfect, and I would love to be working. But do not misunderstand me. I have no regrets for the stand that I took and rejoice at some of the direct fruits of my contention even if I had to be misrepresented and rather cruelly treated because of it.
>
> I might venture here to tell you that God has wonderfully sustained me in all of this controversy. I have come through it with no bitterness or personal resentment. My only feeling is a great heaviness of heart at the attitude of some people and . . . the downright ungodly way in which they sought to carry their point and discredit an unselfish Colored woman (myself, I mean) who had no other motive than an aspiration for her women's freedom and spiritual enlargement.[26]

The Black women's caucus that met in Lugenia's home in April 1920 discussed not only its desire to "integrate the YWCA" but also the possibility that "the time was ripe [to] go beyond the YWCA and any other organization and reach a few outstanding white and Negro women, Christian and with well-balanced judgement and not afraid." The intention of this group was to bring together the strongest and most progressive Black and white leaders in any organization devoted specifically to improving race relations.[27]

At this same time the Methodist Women's Missionary Council was holding its annual meeting in Kansas City, Missouri, and expressing as one of its objectives the desire to bring southern white women into the interracial cooperation movement, a point thoroughly endorsed by the council's president, Belle Bennett, and further endorsed by the guest speaker, Will Alexander of the Commission on Interracial Cooperation (CIC). Though the women of the council had a long history of working with social service programs through the schools and settlement houses in Black communities and in educational programs on race relations in their respective churches, Bennett and Alexander urged them to redirect their efforts into cooperative ventures with Black women on local and regional levels. In response, the council created a commission empowered to "study the whole question of race relationships, the needs of Negro women and children, and methods of cooperation by which better conditions can be brought about."[28]

The opportunity to solicit the support of southern Black women presented itself to Alexander at the dedication of the Butler Street YMCA in Atlanta in 1919. After the ceremony Alexander discussed with Lugenia the Black exodus to the North and the problems facing returning Black soldiers. Both agreed that there was a need for interracial cooperation. He asked her to meet with a group of white women "to discuss phases of the Negro problem and to map out methods of approach." Lugenia accord-

ingly invited two members of the Methodist Women's Missionary
Council, Carrie Parks Johnson (commonly referred to as Mrs.
Luke Johnson) and Sara Estelle Haskin, to her home. At this meet-
ing Lugenia asked the two to attend the biennial conference of the
National Association of Colored Women (NACW) at Tuskegee In-
stitute in July 1920. She then arranged a meeting in Margaret
Murray Washington's home between the two white women and
her southern colleagues.[29]

On arriving at Tuskegee, Haskin and Johnson were offered segregated housing and dining facilities in Dorothy Hall. Their attendance at the first session of the NACW meeting surprised them
because the Black women, who belonged to the rising middle
class, "treated [them] simply as members of the group rather than
as honored white guests." These white women were surprised also
to find that whereas white female leaders often had merely local
and church-related recognition, many of the Black women were
national figures. "Amazed at the intelligence and seriousness of
the delegates," Johnson recalled, "I had a new world opened to
me, a world I had never conceived before." Black attendees included Margaret Washington, Mary McCrorey, M. L. Crosthwait,
Mary M. Bethune, and Lugenia. As they assembled around Booker
T. Washington's teakwood table in his library, "there was an atmosphere of distance, mistrust, and suspicion." The Black women
suspected that the white women's concern for "Negro betterment"
was related to "their desire for more efficient and presentable servants." The inability of the white women to understand the Black
women's anxiety, along with the confusion of etiquette and expec-
tations, threw the participants into a paralyzing discomfort. After
an hour or more of prayer and Scripture reading, both groups
became more frank. The serious discussion commenced with
Lugenia saying: "We have just emerged from a world war that cost
the lives of thousands of our boys fighting to make the world safe
for democracy—For Whom? Women, we can achieve nothing to-

day unless you [who] have met us are willing to help find a place in American life where we can be unashamed and unafraid."[30]

Taking the initiative, Black participants presented their grievances and concerns. The two groups discovered that they had mutual concerns—their children, their homes. Haskin and Johnson asked the women assembled to draw up a statement of their demands. In response, the women made recommendations for improvements in domestic conditions, child welfare, railroad conditions, education, and sanitation; for justice in the courts and fair treatment of Blacks in the press; for the abolition of lynching; and for the extension of the suffrage to all Americans.[31] The most significant portion of the document was its preamble, written by Charlotte Hawkins Brown and Lugenia, which read in part:

> Realizing there is a growing tendency to lay stress upon the influence of the womanhood of the nation; and being fully aware of the very humiliating position which the Negro woman, because of the false estimate of her moral, educational and civic worth, and, regardless of her development, has been forced to occupy; and desiring to secure for her all the privileges and rights granted to American womanhood; for which she is ready because of her training in all activities of American life: Desiring further to create a basis of mutual understanding and cooperation with the white women of the South, because on such cooperation the safety and welfare of both races depends: . . .[32]

Margaret Washington was assigned the task of arranging and typing up the Black women's statement and mailing it to Haskin and Johnson.

This meeting inspired the two white women to petition Alexander for the development of a women's division of the CIC. They wanted to duplicate their experiences at Tuskegee for a larger number of women, thus challenging effectively the "indifference of white-middle-class women and their assumptions of black inferiority." Over the skepticism of fellow male CIC members, Alexander persuaded the body to sponsor a southern women's conference. Female representatives from religious groups, clubs, and the YWCA gathered in a "small dingy room in a Memphis YWCA, where it would be possible to 'control the press' "—a necessity because the situation was "strange and delicate."[33]

Johnson and Haskin opened the meeting by giving an account of what they had discovered at Tuskegee. The audience was told that four Black women from the Tuskegee meeting would speak at the afternoon session—advance notice that allowed any southern white who might object to the presence of Black visitors to exit beforehand. As a further precaution, Alexander and three other men were secreted in a corner where they could oversee the proceedings.

The afternoon session began with conservative and accommodative remarks from Margaret Washington. She recounted her efforts at Tuskegee to educate Black students morally and culturally. She described the inequities of Black education, the difficulties of Black working mothers, and the "system" that destroyed the Black home, although she made it clear that none of these handicaps resulted from any faults of the southern white ladies present. She concluded by calling for a "chance" for cooperation between her group and the southern whites. The speeches of Jennie Moton[34] and Elizabeth Ross Haynes were essentially extensions of Washington's remarks: descriptions of the daily humiliations of life under Jim Crow, with confident assertions that interracial cooperation was a means to alleviate these injustices. The final speaker was Charlotte Hawkins Brown, who began with an account of the dehumanization she had suffered en route to the conference. She was angry that southern white women who witnessed the racism of the railroads merely sat in silence. "I came to Memphis crushed and humiliated," she told her listeners. Brown pursued the theme of the pervasive and oppressive idea of the "promiscuous Black woman," pointing out the terrible assumption that lay behind the discourtesy suffered by Black women: the belief that all Black women were immoral and therefor not entitled to protection from sexual exploitation. Linking Black sexual exploitation with lynching, she challenged the southern white women to confront the evils that Blacks had to confront. Believing that their intercession would produce results, she stated:

> We have become a little bit discouraged. We have begun to feel that you are not after all, interested in us. . . . The Negro women of the South lay everything that happens to the members of [their] race at the door of the Southern white women. . . . We all feel that you can control your men. We feel as far as lynching is concerned that, if the white woman would take hold of the situation, that lynching would be stopped. . . . I want to say to you, when you read in the paper where a colored man has insulted a white woman, just multiply that by one thousand and you have some idea of the number of colored women insulted by white men.
>
> I want to ask . . . won't you help us, friends, to bring to justice the criminal of your race who is just as much [a] criminal when [he] tramps on the womanhood of my race.

She concluded her speech by issuing an appeal for the two groups of Christian women to work together for the good and the survival of both.[35]

Stirred by this speech, the white delegates, far from being angry, "rose to their feet in the ritual response of the evangelical church: heads bowed," and began to sing a familiar hymn of Christian fellowship and solidarity. They promised to help create a "public sentiment" that would sustain officers of the law in deterring lynchings. They adopted a platform based on a statement of grievances drawn up by the Black women at the Tuskegee conference. In addition, the delegates asked the CIC to create a Committee on Women's Work to be funded jointly by the CIC and the Women's Missionary Council. Johnson was chosen to lead the new organization.[36]

Even though the white women pledged their cooperation, a controversy developed immediately. During the Memphis meeting, Carrie Johnson read a version of the Tuskegee statement given to her by Jennie Moton in which "the idea of the preamble had been substantially changed." The clause that claimed for Black women the privileges of American citizenship had been removed. A preface to the anti-lynching resolution added the statement that "we deplore and condemn any act on the part of Negro men which excites the mob spirit."[37]

Though angered by the changes, the Black delegates at first accepted Washington's counsel of silence and moderation. "Let us stand shoulder to shoulder with the two white women and their followers," she admonished. "This Mrs. Johnson, in my mind, is a sincere southern white woman and certainly will need our cooperation and sympathy." She continued: "Let us all try to get our minds on the most important things as relates to our condition, physical, educational, moral, industrial, etc. Every woman in that room that day is [a] well poised woman and we are expected to mark time."[38] Then, however, Johnson indicated that this version of the Black women's statement would be published. An angry Lugenia fired off a series of letters condemning the revisions. She could not understand why part of the preamble should have been deleted, "since this is the Negro woman's viewpoint, and this is what you asked us for, our point of view and not the white woman's point of view." She continued:

> It is difficult for me to understand why my white sisters so strenuously object to this honest expression of colored women as put forth in the discarded preamble. After all when we yield to public opinion and make ourselves say only what we think the public can stand, is there not a danger that we may find ourselves with our larger view conceding what those with the narrow view demand?[39]

The white women, Lugenia observed, "may be too cautious, with too little faith in their own people." She attacked the assumption of racial inferiority that underpinned their objections to the Black preamble. Just how willing were the whites, after all, to have a frank and open statement from independent, thinking Black women? Lugenia summed up her objections:

> Ignorance is ignorance wherever found, yet the most ignorant white woman may enjoy every privilege that America offers. Now I think that the ignorant Negro woman should also enjoy them to the best of her ability. We learn by doing and what is good for one race is good for the other. I therefore cannot understand why this clause should be cut out.[40]

After months of negotiation, the two groups drew up a compromise statement. Yet before it could be submitted for approval by the Black women's caucus, Johnson decided to drop the matter and notified the Black women that there would be no printed pamphlet at all. In a frank letter to Johnson, Lugenia expressed her frustration at being forced to spend an inordinate amount of energy and time in attempts to influence white moderates who were largely outside the mainstream of both political and economic power. In the meantime, "racist demagogues plied their trade, Ku Klux Klaners surged to power, while CIC leaders quibbled over the nuances of wording and used their positions as mediators between the black community and the white power structure to impose their own interpretations of what was strategic and timely on even the most cooperative of black leaders." In contrast, Lugenia added, "the forces of darkness manage to agree about what is 'best for Negroes.'"[41]

Despite this disagreement, the white group went ahead with a follow-up session in Atlanta, with representatives from the Methodist, Baptist, Presbyterian, Episcopal, and Disciples churches and the YWCA. It was months after that before the CIC men would grant them permission to effect a permanent organization. Once established as a committee, the white group voted to include Black women, but it was not until late 1922 that any Black members were actually solicited. Johnson then asked Black women to suggest other Black women as members. Understanding that the white women would be unable to accept any challenge to their leadership, Charlotte Hawkins Brown wrote Mary McLeod Bethune, a member of the Nomination Committee, that since the white committee included only seven women, Blacks should choose only seven also: "If we outnumber them to begin with, we will get no results, you know."[42]

White and Black members of the Women's General Committee were chosen from various denominational groups throughout the South. Church representatives were responsible for disseminating CIC plans in their churches and for seeing that state, district, and local church groups carried out programs designed to improve race relations. On the state level, Black and white women usually formed parallel but separate committees, each having subcommittees on the home, the church, and the school. Members of the executive committees of the white and Black groups formed a joint committee, which met regularly.

White and black women in local committees generally followed the state plan and organized separate committees. Local Black women often suspected white women's motives and feared retaliation from those hostile to interracial work, so getting committees set up proved difficult at times. Lugenia and other Black members faced these fears as they attempted to organize in Georgia. Lugenia's invitation to "outstanding, forward thinking level headed" people from the smaller towns of southwest Georgia met with so much fear and suspicion that she was ultimately able to organize only Black Atlantans.[43]

In 1925 Johnson resigned as the director of women's work of the CIC. She was replaced with Maude Henderson, who formulated a ten-year educational program to improve Black schools in the South. This campaign to improve educational opportunities for Black students had a long history in the region. Atlantans had undertaken the task as early as 1913. With the adoption of the CIC project, the Black women of the women's committee, in conjunction with the International Council of Women of the Darker Races, immediately began to implement their goal of instituting courses in Black history and literature in the schools, both white and Black, private and public. The purpose of this undertaking, organized by Margaret Washington and Lugenia, was not to displace "any other literature or history" but to get all children acquainted with Blacks. "We feel that we can do this if we all pull together," the women's committee instructed the members. "Go at it carefully and thoughtfully in the schools where you have influence." A committee of Black women from both organizations, appointed to develop a curriculum, began by soliciting suggestions of texts from other Blacks; Washington encouraged the group to rely on the work of Carter G. Woodson, "one of our strongest and best writers."[44]

In 1929 Jessie Daniel Ames replaced Henderson as director of women's work of the CIC. Ames shifted the focus of the ten-year program from Black education to the eradication of lynching, and in 1930 she founded a new organization, the Association of Southern Women for the Prevention of Lynching (ASWPL), designed to win for women a greater role in the overall CIC program and to express her own commitment to the anti-lynching cause. Because Ames diverted most of the CIC budget to the work of the ASWPL, all other women's work virtually ceased. By 1937 the central office and/or committee of ASWPL conducted the majority of the fieldwork, since most of the state committees no longer functioned.[45]

Ames's organization was formed during an era that witnessed an increase in lynching. In 1930 thirty-one lynchings were recorded, twenty in the South, and all the victims were Black. The CIC believed that lynching was primarily a means of enforcing economic, political, and racial exploitation, and it took upon itself the role of investigating lynchings and other suspicious deaths in an effort to prevent this type of violence. When a lynching occurred, the CIC collected all available information and gave it to the law enforcement officials. For this purpose the CIC sat up an all-male agency, the Southern Commission on the Study of Lynching. Ames wanted women to be able to assist with the problem of lynching. Her objective was to prevent it, rather than relying on state and local officials to enforce laws that the majority of white people did not believe applied to Blacks.[46]

The ASWPL rejected the pretext that lynching was necessary for the protection of southern white women. Its members saw that lynchings undermined the foundations of society and government, and they lamented the contempt that these crimes brought to the United States from the rest of the world. These middle-class white urbanites organized in rural areas, where most of the lynchings occurred, and they exerted moral and social pressures to persuade women's organizations in these areas to address the issue of lynching. They sincerely believed that public opinion could be educated and changed through their program, which in turn could improve the social welfare and promote interracial goodwill.[47]

Unlike the men of CIC, Ames did not support federal intervention to prevent lynching and never backed any of the anti-lynching bills introduced in Congress. Toward the Costigan-Wagner bill, for example, which proposed federal trials for mob members if local authorities refused to act, fines or jail terms for officers who failed to discharge their duties, and damage claims against counties where lynchings occurred, Ames encouraged all ASWPL members to maintain a policy of neutrality.[48] By 1934 Black women who did support federal intervention became dissatisfied with the silence of the white women and began to voice their discontent, thus revealing a split in the Women's Division of the CIC that was becoming too obvious to be ignored.

To resolve the question whether the ASWPL should continue to oppose federal intervention via the Costigan-Wagner bill, Ames organized a conference between the AWSPL's executive committee and the Black representatives of the Women's Division, many of whom were adamant supporters of organizations (including the NAACP) that endorsed the bill. Black women invited to participate were Daisy Lampkin, NAACP field secretary; Nannie Helen Burroughs, NACW member and founder of the National Training School for Colored Girls; Mary McLeod Bethune; Charlotte Hawkins Brown; and Lugenia. The meeting, held at Atlanta University on January 11, 1935, was opened with a plea from Lampkin for ASWPL's approval of the anti-lynching bill. "Congressional opponents take new courage and they use it to their advantage when they can stand on the floor and say that the . . . southern white women did not endorse the Costigan-Wagner Bill," she told the participants. Her plea was continued by Brown: "Southern women, you can do more . . . to bring about . . . freedom for the Negro race. . . . Congress is controlled by Southerners. . . . I would not have expected you to have done it if the South was not in the saddle."⁴⁹

When it became apparent that the ASWPL leaders were still determined to continue their campaign of education through local committees, and still opposed to federal intervention, Lugenia expressed her frustration and disappointment: "Honestly, my heart is so sick and weak over it that I don't know whether I can say anything. I do think that the stand that the Southern women took will hold back our interracial work and everything else in the South. Because we have just banked so much on it. It is going to be difficult for us to help you explain."⁵⁰ Burroughs noted that she expected the bill to pass whether the ASWPL helped or not. Since Black women were excluded from the ASWPL's membership, they could do nothing to change the organization's course of action anyway. However, she concluded, the AWSPL was nonetheless

justified in continuing its educational campaign. Bethune, closing
the discussion on a conciliatory note, told the white women that
she believed they were wise to be cautious and that she was appreciative of "the daring stand taken by . . . th[is] group of women. I
have only gratitude for what you have done."51

In any survey of the southern Black women's movement, two
themes are paramount: social reform and race consciousness.
While they struggled to provide for Blacks' social and recreational
needs, activist Black southern women also believed that their mission included the raising of the race's political and racial consciousness. Hence they became participants in such groups as the
National Council of Negro Women, the NAACP, and the Urban
League. Projects promoted by these organizations were in part
extensions of ongoing programs inaugurated and led by these
same women on a local or a regional basis. For example, settlement work in Atlanta had been one of the many projects of the
Neighborhood Union since 1908, eight years before the arrival of
the Urban League in the city. As early as 1911, and again in 1913
and 1914, annual reports from the union on community work
and methods of program development were forwarded to the
league's national office in New York. On numerous occasions the
league invited the union to become an affiliate member. As president, Lugenia agreed to share the union's reports but remained
adamant about the organization's independence. She made it clear
to the league's director, Eugene K. Jones, that the union would
neither merge with the league nor totally turn over its community
work in Atlanta to the league.

By 1920 there was much confusion about who began the Black
social work agencies in Atlanta, with the league claiming to have
been involved even before such churches as the First Congregational, which had begun its community work around the turn of
the century. Similarly, female members of other state and city

affiliates, though rarely given the credit, were instrumental in establishing and implementing the goals of national organizations. An example is the Atlanta branch of the NAACP and Lugenia's role in the organization's development. In 1913 W. R. Scott, founder and owner of the Atlanta *Daily World,* requested from the NAACP headquarters information on branch development for the city of Atlanta. By 1916 the branch was established, with Harry H. Pace as president. Between 1916 and 1924 the branch was chartered and reorganized twice, first because of a fire in the headquarters at Bethel AME Church. In 1924 it was reorganized under the leadership of the Reverend A. D. Williams, and the branch again became active as it attacked local problems. For example, it petitioned the Board of Education to protest double sessions in Black public schools and to ask for higher teachers' salaries. Also it continued to aid rural families who were fleeing north via the modern underground railway system to escape peonage in south Georgia. The branch provided these poor families with shelter, food, clothing, and legal aid.[52] In 1925 Williams resigned as branch president, and A. R. Walden, an attorney, was elected. Immediately Walden filed a lawsuit against the Georgia Railway and Power Company, alleging that Black passengers had been assaulted by motormen and conductors. The suit was successful: a fifteen-hundred-dollar settlement was awarded to the NAACP's client.[53]

As a life member and first vice-president of the local branch, Lugenia aided the NAACP Woman's Auxiliary in fund-raising. She supported the Junior Division and delivered many speeches to the youth of the local branch. But her major contribution was in the local branch's effort to educate Black voters. In 1932 the branch established a Citizenship Committee and appointed her as chairperson to "bring about a feeling of race consciousness with . . . reference to the ballot." This committee was responsible for establishing and operating a citizenship school that would "have the courses of instruction so simple, direct and plain that anyone of our group with even a most rudimentary education shall be able to grasp them, thus enabling him to have a comprehensive conception of the functions of our city, county, state, and national governments." The first school session was a series of lectures for ten consecutive weeks on Tuesday nights in Big Bethel Church. Clarence A. Bacote, professor of history at Atlanta University, directed this first series. The response was overwhelming, with over 150 people attending some part of it. Lugenia decided to continue the school for a second term in November 1933. This time Rayford Logan, also of the Department of History at Atlanta University, was the director. Additional schools were operated in various parts of Atlanta over a six-week period each. More than 1,500 persons were in attendance for at least one of the sessions.[54]

The response to the lectures was so positive that the Citizenship Committee created a primer on citizenship, describing the steps in voting on all levels and the qualifications for registering to vote. Sample ballots containing the actual names of district representatives were covered in classes, so that students got instruction both in the mechanics of voting and in the practical politics of choosing the best candidate. Between 1933 and 1934 over two hundred people received certificates. The primer proved so popular that the local branch received numerous requests from schools, civic clubs, and individuals around the country for copies of both the primer and the plan for the citizenship school. As the local report concluded, not only were the school and its primer significant accomplishments for Atlanta, but they had "also won the approval of other cities from coast to coast and aroused in them the desire to follow our lead in preparing their citizens for intelligent voting."[55] Classes continued for several years in Atlanta.

Through her activities with the YWCA, the CIC, and the NAACP, Lugenia demonstrated her commitment to reform and equality.

Her work with the regional and national offices of the YWCA aided the opening of Black branches in the South while putting the national hierarchy straight on the issue of Black participation (something accomplished in no other national women's organization until decades later). Her role in bringing together southern Black and white women contributed to the growth of the interracial movement in the South. Through the NAACP's citizenship schools, established under her supervision, the political consciousness of hundreds of Atlantans was raised. Lugenia the race woman had emerged as a prominent personality in the interracial movement.

Chapter Six

On Her Own

Come sit with me by the fireside
   While the busy world goes by
With its millions wildly striving
   To laugh before they die

For you and me the fever
   of noontime fades away
To you and me the twilight
   Has many things to say.

For we may walk together
   The dim ways of the past
New friends advance and scatter
   Old friends alone will last.

Georgia Douglass Johnson to
Lugenia Burns Hope
(*Washington, D.C., 1937*)

On February 20, 1936, John Hope died from pneumonia at Mac-Vicar Hospital at Spelman. In compliance with his request, he was buried on the main quadrangle of Atlanta University, with the understanding that his wife would be buried beside him if she so desired. In September 1936, only seven months after the death of her husband, Lugenia's sister Ophelia died in Chicago. Thus, within one year, Lugenia lost two immediate family members. Then she was confronted with a forced removal from her home, the presidential house on Beckwith Street. At the insistence of Florence Read, president of Spelman and acting president of Atlanta University, Lugenia was required to vacate the premises earlier than she had expected, and she was not allowed to take any of her personal property. Lugenia moved first into an apartment building on Lee Street where John was living with his wife, Elise. After several months she decided to relocate to New York—her niece Alice Lyons was there—and moved to the YWCA on 137th Street in Harlem.[1]

Why did Lugenia leave Atlanta? The reason for her decision has been buried in some obscurity, not thoroughly clarified by written records or interviews with family members and former colleagues. When Edward was asked, he responded: "I think she did not want to appear to interfere with or inhibit a new administration . . . whose success she was interested in. Later some problems developed and she thought it best if she left." Truly, problems did abound for her. There appears to have been a conflict between her and Florence Read, dating back at least to her husband's illness and subsequent death at Spelman. There was some speculation, not verifiable, that John's wife and sons were not with him when he died and were afterward prevented for a time from entering his room. The resulting bad feeling seems to have triggered Lugenia's removal from the house on Beckwith. Because of this insensitivity, Lugenia was obliged to write to Dean Sage, chairman of the Board of Trustees of Atlanta University, and to Eleanor Roosevelt, the first lady of the United States, in order to secure her personal belongings.[2]

Lugenia's desire not to interfere may have been connected with her firm belief that the incoming president was incompetent, her support for another candidate, and her fear for the quality of instruction at Atlanta University. Former colleague Clarence A.

Bacote, while masterfully avoiding any specifics, did acknowledge that she was "very bitter when she left Atlanta."[3] This bitterness was strong enough so that she made close associates from the Neighborhood Union promise to carry out her instructions to have her ashes thrown over Morehouse and not buried on Atlanta University's campus. Her feelings kept her away from Atlanta for the rest of her life, except for brief visits to her son John before he accepted a position at Fisk University in Nashville; her only interest in Atlanta University between 1936 and 1947 was the condition of her husband's grave and memory at Atlanta University and the university's acquisition of a granite slab to mark the actual grave site.

By 1937 Lugenia was living in New York. Old friends saw to it that she was constantly busy and useful. Then she got an invitation that enabled her to resume her public activism: she was asked to become administrative assistant to Mary M. Bethune in her residentially appointed position as Director of Negro Affairs of the National Youth Administration (NYA). For the next year Lugenia traveled with Bethune and other assistants across the United States, giving speeches and investigating NYA branches. In 1938 she sent the agenda of an upcoming tour to Lloyd Lewis, the husband of her niece Emma. The tour would last from April 6 until May 20, with scheduled stops in Milwaukee, Phoenix, Des Moines, San Francisco, Los Angeles, Albuquerque, Wichita, Tulsa, Langston (Oklahoma), Oklahoma City, Topeka, Kansas City, and finally Washington, D.C. Commenting on her role on the tour, Lugenia told Lewis that "the man will look after all the details and we shall only have to talk and I will look wise avoiding all of the talks possible." By May 15 the tour was in Hot Springs, Arkansas; from there she wrote her nephew Earl Burns that her neuritis was bothering her "because of that old cold house" (the president's home on Beckwith), and she had decided to stay on for ten days.[4]

By 1940 Lugenia's health was beginning to fail. Nevertheless, her life continued to be dominated by numerous affiliations, memberships, and career involvements, and she still traveled extensively. She served on the National Advisory Council of the National Association of Colored Graduate Nurses, an association launched in 1934 by Mabel Staupers to secure scholarships and training opportunities for Black nurses. Throughout 1943, Lugenia attended the organization's meetings and conferences with Staupers and the racial activist Anna Arnold Hedgemen.[5] She continued to support the NAACP, endorsing its programs and periodically traveling to Washington, D.C., to testify before Congress in support of some measure in its fight for Black equality. During the war years she became a member and attended meetings of the Women's Interracial Committee of the Federal Council of Churches of Christ in America. She served on the Executive Council of the American Women's Volunteer Services until she learned of its policy of discrimination. For several years she lectured throughout the country for the National Council of Negro Women. Until 1942 she was chairperson of the council's Citizenship Committee, of which Bethune was founder and president. When Lugenia resigned, for health reasons, Bethune responded: "Your resignation is before me. I do not question resignations when they come. I always feel that those who are offering them usually understand why. I can only say how deeply I regret to have this. . . . I hope . . . that . . . you will have recovered your strength sufficiently to give another interpretation to your ability to serve the Council."[6]

While Lugenia remained in sufficient health, she attended luncheons, conferences, dinners, and meetings with old and new friends and acquaintances like W. E. B. Du Bois, John W. Davis, Paul Robeson, and Channing Tobias, and with family members: Emma and Lloyd, John and Elise, Edward and his wife, Marion, and niece Alice. She also undertook two projects concerning her husband. By 1943 World War II had reached Atlanta University.

Troops were stationed there, marching constantly around the campus. Fearing that her husband's unmarked grave was being trampled, Lugenia contacted Dean Sage. After conferring with Read, Sage was able to assure Lugenia that the grave was not being desecrated, that John Hope's memory was very much alive in the Atlanta University Center, that a granite slab had been ordered for the grave site, and that the school had planned a ceremony when the marker arrived. At the dedication John Hope III, the son of John II, unveiled the slab over his famous grandfather's grave.[7]

Secondly, after a family consultation, Lugenia agreed to cooperate with Ridgely Torrence on a biography of her husband. She asked Torrence, a white man, how he intended to portray John. If he meant to capture the true spirit of her husband, she told Torrence, "This book ought to be an expression of the race problem." She questioned whether his work would be censored by his editors: "you state facts about the white race—will it be cut out—if it is, the soul of the book will be lost." She told Torrence that her husband never felt that he was making any sacrifices for his race. "Because he was thrown with white boys all through his educational life it never changed his feeling for his own people. Practically all of his close friends were dark folk." Again she challenged Torrence, "Your book could be a best seller if you write into it as much of the truth as you can absorb." But she did not live to see if his published book met her standards; *The Story of John Hope* appeared in 1948, the year after her death.[8]

By 1944 Lugenia's health was rapidly declining. Many of her activities were curtailed during illnesses and while she underwent treatments at the Mayo Clinic, Wedworth Hospital, and Harlem Hospital. On several occasions she left her home to attend a function only to have to return and rest. In January 1944, on the morning she was to christen the liberty ship *John Hope,* she suffered a stroke as she prepared to leave home. For weeks she remained in Harlem Hospital. Once she was ready for travel, she went to Chicago and then Atlanta in the company of a nurse and a physician. In 1945 she returned to Chicago to live with Emma and Lloyd, who had renovated their home to accommodate her. Thereafter she varied her residence by going to stay with John and Elise in Nashville or Edward and Marion in Washington, D.C.[9] During her visits to John and Elise, Lugenia would periodically check herself into Nashville's Riverside Sanitarium, and there, in June 1947, she began receiving treatment for a heart problem. She would spend several weeks with John and then return to the hospital to rest. In August she was able to convince John and Elise to take their planned vacation to Rochester, Minnesota. While they were away, during the evening of the fourteenth of August, she died of heart failure.

In compliance with her wishes, her body was cremated and a funeral ceremony was conducted in John's home in Nashville. In November Morehouse College held a memorial service. Before the service, again in accordance with her wishes, and to prevent the presidents of Atlanta University and Morehouse College from burying her ashes beside her husband's grave on Atlanta University property, several members of the Neighborhood Union secretly climbed the tower of Graves Hall and scattered her remains "to the four winds" over the campus of "the House."[10]

The memorial service consisted of musical selections performed by the Morehouse Quartet and by the choir of her church, Friendship Baptist. Her pastor, the Reverend Maynard H. Jackson, Sr., presided. Lloyd Lewis delivered a family statement, and four people who had worked with and respected Lugenia gave eulogies addressing various aspects of her life: Ira de A. Reid of Atlanta University spoke on "Mrs. Hope in the Life of Morehouse College"; Walter Chivers of Morehouse College on "Mrs. Hope and the Atlanta Community"; her lifelong friend and colleague Charlotte Hawkins Brown on "Mrs. Hope in the National Scene"; and Morehouse's president, Benjamin E. Mays, on "The Woman."[11] Thus the seventy-six-year-old race woman returned to the place she had said she "loved the best in the world,"[12] Morehouse College.

Chapter Seven

"For the Ladies or For Colored People?": An Overview

This examination of the life of Lugenia Burns Hope has revealed her as a representative of several aspects of Afro-American, American, and women's histories.[1] Lugenia continued the tradition of Black women who founded and nurtured services needed in the Black community. She represented a group of Black women who were members of a privileged class, yet who used their time, influence, prestige, and contacts to advance their race.[2] These middle-class American women were multifaceted in purpose and action; conscious of the claims of community, race, sex, children, and the poor, they participated actively in various social service organizations whose goals were moral and racial uplift, intraracial cooperation, racial and sexual equality, and social and civic improvements. Lugenia represented the segment of this group that was independent, outspoken, assertive—even aggressive—but submissive when it was expedient to be so.

These women were not only activists but also mothers, wives, and educators. Cognizant of their sexuality as well as the sexual discrimination against them, these southern Victorians were nonetheless as reluctant as their New England counterparts to acknowledge a sexual consciousness. They sublimated this awareness into the conviction that femininity and domesticity should govern human relations. In this respect Lugenia was typical of the Progressive female reformer—black or white—in the early decades of the twentieth century. These reformers challenged vice, corruption, and injustice on most levels. They sought social justice and municipal reforms by supporting Prohibition, woman suffrage, and public ownership of utility companies; by working to rid the streets of prostitution and to end child labor and abuse; and by creating day-care centers and kindergartens for the children of working mothers.

But Black and white college-educated female reformers differed on the inclusion of sexual and racial issues on their respective agendas. They differed, as well, in the reasons why they became reformers.[3] Those white female college graduates of the early 1900s who wanted public lives had two options: the continuation of their studies in graduate programs where social issues were neutral or entrance into professional careers of social activism. For those who chose the latter, activism became a way of curing the emotional prostration that afflicted women in the Victorian era. The initial impulse for "feminine migration to the slums was not identification with the working class . . . but the recognition that there was a social cure for the neurotic ills of privileged young women in America . . . [with] ailments [that] were socially induced." It was to release this "nervous energy," as well as to confront social evils, that women like Jane Addams and Lillian Ward organized settlement houses and homes for delinquent or working girls. It was common in this period for white women activists to define men as less Christian in spirit than women and as motivated to action entirely by commercial rewards. Becoming social critics of urban industrial America, the women of this group saw themselves as the only truly democratic force in society and the only one to understand that the perils of American poverty were the results of masculine exploitation. They endorsed biological

and evolutionary theories that held women to be innately nurturing and passive instead of warlike and aggressive. They emerged
in their own view as popular heroines, sages, and prophetesses.[4]
Black educated female reformers were mostly educators or social workers and organizers of settlement work, community building, day-care centers and kindergartens, campaigns to get the vote
for Black men and women, anti-lynching campaigns, Prohibition,
and similar causes. These Black women also believed in the moral
superiority of the female, but they did not hold their men in the
same contempt. Whereas white female leaders tended to be spin-
sters, their Black counterparts were often married—many of them
to prominent race men of the era—and many of them had children. Black women reformers were also opposed to warlike and
aggressive action at home and abroad, especially the mob rule that
was prevalent in the South. To promote peace and worldwide harmony some of them organized the International Council of
Women of the Darker Races, which met regularly during the
twenties and thirties. Black female reformers became national
spokespersons for societal changes by challenging factors that
limited them as women and especially as Blacks. They founded
their own female associations or worked within traditional race
organizations in order to effect change. They emerged not only as
Progressives but even more as race people.

Lugenia exemplified the strongest-spirited of these reformers.
Throughout her career she showed herself to be a determined
woman who recognized and utilized her abilities and who expected the same from others. Her values were firm, and she
worked unrelentingly to reach lofty goals. She succeeded as a
leader because of her ability to work with a diversity of people and
groups and her immense executive capacity. Part of her appeal
was her genuine love and concern for all children and her willingness to struggle to improve their lives. Another part was her organizational expertise, which again and again caused her to be asked

to provide advice and chair committees. The organization of the Neighborhood Union, which brought together her concerns and her strengths, demonstrated her skills. By dividing the city into zones, the zones into districts, and the districts into neighborhoods, the plan of organization called for directed community involvement. Because neighborhood members elected their immediate neighborhood presidents, and these presidents were automatically members of the Board of Managers, each community's input into the overall planning of the program was guaranteed.

Few accounts, written or oral, assess the reaction of the community, or of fellow union members, to Lugenia's leadership. From oral testimonies of descendants of union founders and early members, one can conclude that Lugenia was held in high regard and that the community tended to defer to her opinions. The minutes of the Neighborhood Union reflect her domination throughout her years of active service. Her position in the community and her middle-class status meant prestige and influence. Community residents looked to her for guidance and expected her, because she was Mrs. John Hope and a woman of education, experience, and social grace, to represent their grievances before such authorities as the Board of Education and the City Council.

Though committed to improving the quality of life for Black Atlantans, Lugenia was, as noted, also a product of Victorian America. She accepted the moral values of the era, and one of her reasons for joining the Black clubwomen's movement was a sense of conscious superiority to those less-fortunate sisters who were the primary representatives of the Black woman in contemporary literature. Lugenia, like her colleagues, wanted to encourage the dominant white class to take notice of an educated Black middle class. This group defined what was morally and racially appropriate by using its own standards as guidelines. Those whose examples did not represent "clean living" became victims of moral cleanups. Since the purpose of these campaigns was to save the youngsters, little attention was paid to persons who were judged undesirable and summarily uprooted (though often only to move to another Black street or section). Few projects were initiated to assist those whose objectionable behavior had called them to the attention of the reformers.

In the radical style of her activism, Lugenia was less like her peers. Compared to her contemporaries, she was more outspoken and more demanding in her campaign for racial justice. This directness may have resulted partly from the influence of her husband, who was also very active as a reformer. It may have been triggered in part by her move to the Deep South, which confronted her with the region's blatant racism. It may also have been in some ways a compensation for the lack of racial consciousness shown by some members of her family, who opted to "pass." Whatever its other sources, however, her radicalism must have been an inherent part of her personality, a force that enhanced her commitment to improving the quality of life for Black southern youngsters. Once she had located in Atlanta, Lugenia referred to her reform activities as a continuation of her earlier work in Chicago. Nonetheless, she became more accusatory and direct and less conciliatory, particularly in interracial meetings, than most of her colleagues. Her philosophy, as Charlotte Hawkins Brown put it in her remarks at Lugenia's memorial service, was "Better not try at all, than sacrifice any of the higher values necessary for genuine respect of womanhood without regard to color or race." Lugenia operated, Brown continued,

frankly and forthrightly . . . , almost belligerently, and at times it caused clashes, [but] it was the only way to freedom and understanding. . . . She despised deceit and camouflage on the part of anyone in either group. I can hear her saying now, "Charlotte . . . we must not let that pass, if we do we shall meet it again." And on through the years, this uncompromising yet kind and tender hearted woman fought through the night of our experience for some of the . . . ground we have gained in human relations.[5]

Earlier, in the tribute offered to Lugenia at the Neighborhood Union's twenty-fifth anniversary, Mary M. Bethune had also acknowledged the impatience Lugenia felt because "our steps up the dizzy heights had to be taken so slowly and with such painstaking deliberation." She added, however, that Lugenia's peers looked upon her "with great admiration for her dauntless courage and her untiring effort in helping to find a way to eradicate prejudice and injustice. . . . [A]t the most intense moment, the purity of her motive has always shone crystal clear; the fairness of her method has been unquestioned; and the wisdom of her procedure has been justified by ultimate results."[6]

Whether Lugenia's steadfastness and forthrightness were realistic during the accommodation era of Booker T. Washington is debatable. But she did present an alternative to southern whites, who generally accepted the conciliatory views of conservative Blacks. Though these views frequently dominated interracial work, and though on many occasions Lugenia bowed to them in order to promote racial harmony, her voice of opposition did assist the growth of racial cooperation in the South.

Lugenia's impact on the lives of Black Atlantans has been the essential focus of this life story. She was more instrumental than has been generally recognized in helping Black Atlanta attain its goals and aims during the first half of the twentieth century. In many campaigns her role was pivotal: improving the health care of Black children and adults in Atlanta, raising the level of education in Atlanta's Black public schools, teaching Black Atlantans about government and citizenship through the citizenship schools of the NAACP, providing safe recreational facilities for Atlanta's Black children, and persuading the YWCA to organize Black branches in the South on a basis of equality. Her commitments went far beyond a peripheral status, and she was present at meetings usually on her own behalf, not as an emissary for her husband. The account of Lugenia's life is an essential component in the wider story of Black community organizing. Racism and sexism have limited the availability of knowledge about the lives and works of such leaders, but Lugenia's story will illustrate those collective activities of southern Black women, and Black women in general, whose struggles have immensely affected our social and cultural history.

Notes

Introduction

1 · "Minutes of the Conference," undated, YWCA Folder, Neighborhood Union Collection (hereafter cited as NUC), Atlanta University Center-Woodruff Library.

2 · "Mrs. Hope on the Cleveland Meeting," May 20, 1920, YWCA Folder, NUC.

3 · For more detail on the YWCA campaign, see chapter 5.

4 · "Race women" and "race men" were terms used early in the twentieth century to designate those Blacks who were actively promoting racial progress and struggling for racial equality.

5 · Sadie I. Daniel, *Women Builders* (Washington, D.C.: Associated Publishers, 1931), p. 1–27.

6 · Quoted in ibid., p. 24.

7 · Sharon Harley, "Black Women in a Southern City: Washington, D.C., 1890–1920," in Joanne V. Hawks and Sheild L. Skemp (eds.), *Sex, Race, and the Role of Women in the South* (Jackson: University Press of Mississippi, 1983), pp. 72–73. See also Dolores Janiewski, "Sisters under Their Skins: Southern Working Women, 1880–1950," in ibid., pp. 13–15.

8 · According to Jacqueline Jones, *Labor of Love, Labor of Sorrow: Black Women, Work, and the Family from Slavery to the Present* (New York: Basic Books, 1985), pp. 110–51, Black urban women worked during this period as washerwomen, laundresses, seamstresses, and dressmakers, as well as sellers of flowers, fruits, and vegetables during off periods to augment family incomes.

9 · *Southern Negro Women and Race Co-operation,* a pamphlet of the Southeastern Federation of Colored Women's Clubs, October 20–22, 1920, Commission on Interracial Cooperation Folder, NUC; Harley, "Black Women in a Southern City," pp. 89–91.

10 · Deborah G. White, "The Lives of Slave Women," *Southern Exposure* 12 (November/December 1984): 32–39. See also White's *Ar'n't I a Woman? Female Slaves in the Plantation South* (New York: W. W. Norton and Co., 1985).

11 · Eugene Levy, *James Weldon Johnson: Black Leader, Black Voice* (Chicago: University of Chicago Press, 1973), pp. 45–47.

12 · Quoted in ibid., p. 48.

13 · Bell Hooks, *Ain't I a Woman: Black Women and Feminism* (Boston: South End Press, 1981), pp. 161–64; Paula Giddings, *When and Where I Enter: The Impact of Black Women on Race and Sex in America* (New York: William Morrow and Co., 1984), pp. 119–31.

Chapter One

1 · "Biographical Statement of Joseph Burns," Emma Bryant Lewis Papers, a division of the Lloyd Lewis Collection (hereafter cited as LLC), Manuscript Division, University of Illinois, Chicago Circle Campus. For information on the public career of William Burns, Sr., see Personal Folder, Drawer 12, Manuscript Division, Mississippi State Archives and Records, Jackson.

2 · "Biographical Statement of Joseph Burns," LLC. The history of race relations in Natchez, Miss., is unique. Many of the horrors of slavery were avoided in Natchez because of the extensive intermixture of the races. Mulattoes of these interracial unions were extremely conscious of their white heritage. Many preferred to pass as white, and those who remained Black also tended to define themselves by the amount of white blood they had inherited. This was the situation with the Berthas and the Burnses. Both families were free Blacks who lived openly with their white male members. In fact, the free Berthas believed themselves superior to their white half-sister and -brother: after all, the brother was an overseer, a position reserved for the poor white class.

3 · The U.S. Census for 1870 also lists Redford and William III as two of Ferdinand and Louisa's older children. Both children died young, and little information has survived.

4 · The term "pre-migration period" refers to the years 1870 to 1915. For a discussion of the Great Migration of Blacks into Chicago, a movement viewed with disdain by the Old Settlers, see St. Clair Drake and Horace R.

Cayton, *Black Metropolis: A Study of Negro Life in a Northern City*, vol. 1 (New York: Harcourt, Brace and World, 1970), chaps. 1–3.

5 · Ibid.

6 · Ibid., pp. 46–54, chaps. 13, 19–21.

7 · Ibid., p. 48. See also *Crusade for Justice: The Autobiography of Ida B. Wells*, ed. Alfreda M. Duster (Chicago: University of Chicago Press, 1970).

8 · Wells, *Crusade for Justice;* Drake and Cayton, *Black Metropolis,* p. 48.

9 · Drake and Cayton, *Black Metropolis,* pp. 72–76.

10 · Personal notes of Lugenia Burns Hope, Biographical Folder, John and Lugenia Burns Hope Papers (hereafter cited as JLBH), Atlanta University Center-Woodruff Library; Chicago Art Institute, school catalog and student records for 1891–92, official transcript of L. D. Burns, and personal interview with Mary McIssac, Office of the Registrar, August 11, 1982.

11 · "Biographical Statement of Mrs. John Hope," NUC.

12 · Personal notes of Lugenia Burns Hope, Biographical Folder, JLBH.

13 · Lugenia Burns went with Warne to Hull House to volunteer her services to Addams. She was Warne's assistant while working there, and through Warne was introduced to Jane Addams. She was influenced by the settlement work at Hull House and she admired Addams, though the two did not work together on Hull House projects: Addams's work, not necessarily Addams herself, was the influence. Records do not reflect any contact between the two after the original introduction, though they probably did see each other at various meetings of the NAACP, since both worked with that organization.

14 · "Biographical Statement of Mrs. John Hope," NUC.

15 · Wells, *Crusade for Justice,* p. 117.

16 · Ridgely Torrence, *The Story of John Hope* (New York: Macmillan Co., 1948), pp. 102–3.

Chapter Two

1 · John Hope to Lugenia Burns, August 19, 1896, Family Folder, JLBH.

2 · Lugenia Burns to John Hope, August 20, 1896, ibid.

3 · Ibid.; John Hope to Lugenia Burns, September 1896 and undated, ibid.

4 · John Hope to Lugenia Burns, September 27, 1896, and undated, ibid.

5 · John Hope to Lugenia, undated, ibid.

6 · John Hope to Lugenia Burns, December 8 and 16, 1896, and undated, ibid.; Lugenia Burns to John Hope, December 4 and 20, 1896, and undated, LLC.

7 · John Hope to Lugenia Burns, December 6 and 8, 1896, Family Folder, JLBH.

8 · Torrence, *The Story of John Hope,* pp. 120–21.

9 · Ibid.

10 · For the history of Morehouse College, see Benjamin Brawley, *The History of Morehouse College* (Atlanta: Morehouse College, 1917); and Edward A. Jones, *A Candle in the Dark: A History of Morehouse College* (Valley Forge, Pa.: Judson Press, 1967).

11 · Jones, *A Candle in the Dark,* pp. 58, 74–75; Brawley, *The History of Morehouse College,* pp. 71, 88–89.

12 · Hope Folder, LLC. For further discussion on the day-care and kindergarten histories of Atlanta, see Louie D. Shivery, "The History of Organized Social Work among Negroes in Atlanta, 1890–1935" (M.A. thesis, Atlanta University, 1936), chap. 2; Mabel Glover Logan, "A Developmental History of the Gate City Day Nursery Association, Atlanta, Georgia" (M.A. thesis, Atlanta University, 1955); "The Gate City Free Kindergarten," NUC; and personal interview with Mae Harvey, Atlanta, March 14, 1982. Mrs. Harvey is the daughter of Ida Wynn and has in her possession a handwritten historical account of the Gate City Free Kindergarten Association; a duplicate of this document is also housed at the Atlanta Historical Society.

13 · For a complete discussion of the environment surrounding Atlanta Baptist College and the community work that gave rise to the Neighborhood Union, see chapter 4.

14 · Personal notes of Mrs. John Hope, untitled folder, JLBH.

15 · Hope Folder, LLC; Personal notes of Mrs. John Hope, untitled folder, JLBH. Gerda Lerner suggests that these women began to define their aim as the "moral, economic and social advancement of Negroes in Atlanta" as early as 1901, even though Lerner does not use this early date. See her "Early Community Work of Black Club Women," *Journal of Negro History* 59 (April 1974): 158–67.

16 · For a discussion of the Hopes as the first family of Atlanta Baptist College, see chapter 3.

17 · Personal interview with Dr. John Hope II, retired economist, youn-

gest son of Lugenia and John Hope, Washington, D.C., August 10, 1982; "Mrs. John Hope: My Mother," a document written expressly for the author by the oldest son of Lugenia and John Hope, Dr. Edward S. Hope, Sr., a retired civil engineer, Cleveland, Ohio, p. 4.

18 · Personal interview with John Hope II, August 18, 1982.

19 · Personal interviews with John Hope II, July 27, 1981, and August 18, 1982.

20 · Edward Hope, "My Mother," p. 4.

21 · Folder 1917, NUC.

22 · Torrence, *The Story of John Hope,* p. 166; Edward Hope, "My Mother," pp. 1–4.

23 · Ibid., p. 5.

24 · Personal interviews with Mae Harvey, the club's historian, daughter of Ida Wynn and widow of Coach B. T. Harvey of Morehouse College, Atlanta, February 13 and March 10, 1982; personal interview with Vivian Beavers, club member, Atlanta, January 22, 1982. It was John Hope who suggested the club's name; it had been the name of a study group he chaired as a student at Brown University. The club adopted the name, chose brown and blue as its colors, and took a ring enclosing a question mark as its emblem. Membership was limited to twelve, with vacancies restricted to daughters or daughters-in-law of the original members. Lugenia eventually brought her daughter-in-law Elise, John's wife, into the club.

25 · Torrence, *The Story of John Hope,* pp. 312–13; John Hope to Lugenia Burns Hope, 1929, Family Folder, JLBH.

26 · John Hope to Lugenia Burns Hope, undated, Family Folder, JLBH.

27 · John Hope to Lugenia Burns Hope, June 12, 1912, ibid.

28 · John Hope to Lugenia Burns Hope, August 1912, ibid.

29 · Torrence, *The Story of John Hope,* p. 174.

30 · John Hope to Lugenia Burns Hope, August 1931 and August 1933, Family Folder, JLBH.

31 · John Hope to Lugenia Burns Hope, May 12, 1912, ibid.

32 · Edward Hope, "My Mother," pp. 3–4.

33 · Personal interview with Elise O. Hope, Washington, D.C., August 18, 1982.

Chapter Three

1 · For the best coverage of Atlanta's race riot, see Ray Stannard Baker, *Following the Color Line: American-Negro Citizenship in the Progressive Era* (1908; New York: Harper Torchbooks, 1964); Charles Crowe, "Race Violence and Social Reform: Origins of the Atlanta Riot of 1906," *Journal of Negro History* 53 (July 1968): 234–56; and Charles Crowe, "Racial Massacre in Atlanta, September 22, 1906," *Journal of Negro History* 54 (April 1969): 150–73. Other sources examining the period include John Dittmer, *Black Georgia in the Progressive Era, 1900–1920* (Urbana: University of Illinois Press, 1977); Benjamin E. Mays, *Born to Rebel: An Autobiography* (New York: Charles Scribner's Sons, 1971); Hollis R. Lynch, *The Black Urban Condition: A Documentary History, 1866–1971* (New York: Thomas Y. Crowell Co., 1973); Thomas H. Deaton, "Atlanta during the Progressive Era" (Ph.D. dissertation, University of Georgia, 1969); Henry H. Proctor, *Between Black and White: Autobiographical Sketches* (1925; New York: Viking Press, 1948); Benjamin J. Davis, *Communist Councilman from Harlem: Autobiographical Notes Written in a Federal Penitentiary* (New York: International Publishers, 1969); Angelo Herndon, *Let Me Live* (New York: Random House, 1937); Charles Martin, *The Angelo Herndon Case and Southern Justice* (Baton Rouge: Louisiana State University Press, 1976); Alton Hornsby, Jr. (ed.), *In the Cage: Eyewitness Accounts of the Freed Negro in Southern Society, 1877–1929* (Chicago: Quadrangle Books, 1971); and Clarence A. Bacote, "Some Aspects of Negro Life in Georgia, 1880–1908," *Journal of Negro History* 43 (Winter 1958): 186–213.

2 · Deaton, "Atlanta during the Progressive Era," p. 186; Baker, *Following the Color Line,* pp. 3–5. See also Atlanta *News,* July 1, 1906, p. 1.

3 · Atlanta *Constitution,* August 6, 1906, p. 1.

4 · Walter White, *A Man Called White* (New York: Macmillian Co., 1948), pp. 5–6.

5 · Atlanta *News,* September 22, 1906, p. 1, and September 23, 1906, p. 1.

6 · Atlanta *News,* August 26, 1906, p. 1; Lynch, *The Black Urban Condition,* pp. 56–58.

7 · Personal recollections of Lugenia Hope, possibly the beginning of her memoirs, undated, untitled, written on calendar pages for 1944–45, Hope Folder, LLC. Ridgely Torrence corroborates the fact that John Hope

and a Black professor patrolled the campus: "Then they were displaced by the militia, among whom they recognized faces from the mob of the night before. A graduate of Atlanta Baptist College recollected that President Hope did approach a white soldier. The soldier cried out: 'What do you want? Put your hands up!' Hope put up his hands but continued walking toward the soldier, who pointed a gun. Hope stopped and with a smile invited him into the house for a cup of coffee. The man lowered his gun and came in." *The Story of John Hope,* p. 153. Edward Hope remembered that Lugenia arranged for coffee to be taken to the soldiers who finally came to guard the campus. "My Mother," pp. 3–4.

8 · Interview with Dr. Samuel H. Nabrit, former student at Morehouse College, Atlanta, April 12, 1975, as cited in Anne Beard, "Mrs. John Hope: Community Builder in Atlanta, Georgia, 1900–1936" (M.A. thesis, Atlanta University, 1975), p. 9; Personal interview with Dr. Melvin Watson, former student at Morehouse College, Atlanta, March 23, 1982; interview with Dr. Brailsford Brazeal, former student and academic dean, Morehouse College, Atlanta, April 21, 1975, as cited in Beard, "Mrs. John Hope," p. 10; interview with Dr. Edward Jones, former student at Morehouse College, Atlanta, May 7, 1980, as cited in ibid.; Edward Hope, "My Mother," p. 2; interview with the Reverend William H. Borders, former student at Morehouse College, Atlanta, June 5, 1975, as cited in Beard, "Mrs. John Hope," p. 10.

9 · Brazeal interview in Beard, "Mrs. John Hope," pp. 12–13.

10 · Neighborhood Union, Folders 1912–1914 and 1916–1918, NUC.

11 · Beard, "Mrs. John Hope," pp. 11–12; "Morehouse Holds Memorial Service for Mrs. Hope," Morehouse *Alumnus,* March–April 1948, p. 10.

12 · Shivery, "History of Organized Social Work among Negroes in Atlanta," pp. 184–87.

13 · Beard. "Mrs. John Hope," pp. 12–13; Jones, *A Candle in the Dark,* p. 257; personal interview with Mrs. Sarah Green, formerly of the History Department, Morehouse College, Atlanta, October 18, 1982. At present two of the auxiliary's annual fund-raising activities are the fall and spring bake and book sales in Benjamin E. Mays Hall.

14 · Edward Hope, "My Mother," pp. 3, 6.

15 · Torrence, *The Story of John Hope,* chap. 17.

16 · Neighborhood Union, Folder 1934–1935, NUC.

17 · Personal interview with John Hope II, August 18, 1982; Edward Hope, "My Mother," p. 8.

18 · Torrence, *The Story of John Hope,* pp. 358–61.

19 · Lugenia's personal handwritten recollections of her talks with Torrence, possibly materials to be incorporated into her memoirs, undated, untitled, Hope Folder, LLC.

20 · For descriptions of influential Black women of the era, see Joseph J. Boris (ed.), *Who's Who in Colored America: A Biographical Dictionary of Notable Living Persons of Negro Descent in America,* vol. 1 (New York: Who's Who in Colored America Corp., 1927).

Chapter Four

1 · Dittmer, *Black Georgia in the Progressive Era,* pp. 12–22.

2 · See Mary F. Berry, "Repression of Blacks in the South, 1890–1945: Enforcing the System of Segregation," in Robert Haws (ed.), *The Age of Segregation: Race Relations in the South, 1890–1945* (Jackson: University Press of Mississippi, 1978), pp. 28–32.

3 · Clarence A. Bacote, "The Negro in Atlanta Politics," *Phylon* 16 (Fourth Quarter 1955): 339–43; Howard N. Rabinowitz, *Race Relations in the Urban South, 1865–1890* (New York: Oxford University Press, 1978), pp. 282–304, 318–19; Dittmer, *Black Georgia in the Progressive Era,* pp. 95–97. Rayford Logan analyzes the deterioration of race relations and the economic and social status of Blacks at the turn of the century in *The Betrayal of the Negro: From Rutherford B. Hayes to Woodrow Wilson* (New York: Collier Books, 1970).

4 · Jones, *Labor of Love, Labor of Sorrow,* pp. 111, 142–46; Dittmer, *Black Georgia in the Progressive Era,* p. 13; August Meier and David Lewis, "History of the Negro Upper Class in Atlanta, Georgia, 1890–1958," *Journal of Negro Education* 28 (Spring 1959): 128–39.

5 · Janiewski, "Sisters under Their Skins," pp. 20–35.

6 · Dittmer, *Black Georgia in the Progressive Era,* pp. 50–71, 112–13, 119–20; Rabinowitz, *Race Relations in the Urban South,* pp. 282–304, 329–39; Michael L. Porter, "Black Atlanta: An Interdisciplinary Study of Blacks on the East Side of Atlanta, 1890–1930" (Ph.D. dissertation, Emory University, 1974), pp. 90, 108.

7 · Porter, "Black Atlanta," p. 90. See also Deaton, "Atlanta during the Progressive Era," p. 171.

8 · Dorothy Slade, "The Evolution of Negro Areas in the City of Atlanta" (M.A. thesis, Atlanta University, 1946), pp. 24–25; Shivery, "History of Organized Social Work among Negroes in Atlanta," pp. 75–76; Porter, "Black Atlanta," pp. 106–9; Deaton, "Atlanta during the Progressive Era," p. 172.

9 · Deaton, "Atlanta during the Progressive Era," p. 174.

10 · Baker, *Following the Color Line,* p. 7.

11 · Slade, "Evolution of Negro Areas in Atlanta," pp. 76–77; Porter, "Black Atlanta," p. 110.

12 · Ibid, p. 100.

13 · Deaton, "Atlanta during the Progressive Era," p. 174; Franklin M. Garrett, *Atlanta and Environs: A Chronicle of Its People and Events,* vol. 2 (New York: Lewis Historical Publishing Co., 1954), p. 607.

14 · Deaton, "Atlanta during the Progressive Era," pp. 175–79; Porter, "Black Atlanta," p. 91. For an examination of the community of Reynoldstown, see Maggie M. Gilead, "Reynoldstown: A Search for Community" (Ph.D. dissertation, Emory University, 1981).

15 · Slade, "Evolution of Negro Areas in Atlanta," pp. 77–79.

16 · Porter, "Black Atlanta," pp. 70–72; Proctor, *Between Black and White,* pp. 107–8; Atlanta *Independent,* August 29, 1908, p. 1, September 10, 1910, p. 3, and August 15, 1914, p. 2. For in-depth studies of the role of the church as a social agency, see Louise E. Torrence, "Social Activities of the Negro Church in Atlanta, Georgia" (M.A. thesis, Atlanta University, 1934); Merlissie Ross Middleton, "Residential Distribution of Members of an Urban Church" (M.A. thesis, Atlanta University, 1953); and David A. Russell, Jr., "The Institutional Church in Transition: A Study of the First Congregational Church of Atlanta, Georgia" (M.A. thesis, Atlanta University, 1971).

17 · Shivery, "History of Organized Social Work among Negroes in Atlanta," p. 43.

18 · Ibid., pp. 43–44; Beard, "Mrs. John Hope," pp. 10–12; E. Franklin Frazier, "The Neighborhood Union in Atlanta," *Southern Workman* 51 (September 1923): 437.

19 · Frazier, "The Neighborhood Union," pp. 438, 442. See also Minutes of Meetings, Folders 1908, 1909, and 1910, NUC; "Atlanta Thanks College Women for Community Service Center," Chicago *Defender,* Oc-

tober 31, 1935, p. 1; "Treating Negro Program at Basis," Atlanta *Constitution,* undated, NUC.

20 · Minutes of Meetings, Folder 1934–1935, NUC; "Report of the Emergency Committee of Neighborhood Union," Folder 1935, NUC.

21 · Shivery, "History of Organized Social Work among Negroes in Atlanta," p. 53.

22 · Ibid., pp. 45–47.

23 · *Neighborhood Union of Atlanta, Georgia* (pamphlet), NUC; Neighborhood Union Constitution, Folder 1908, NUC; "Plans of Organization," undated document, Folder 1917, NUC. In 1909 the union added an Advisory Board of eleven men to assist in "stamping out anything that tends to injure the morals of the community." Later minutes reveal that men were active members of the union by the 1920s and were instrumental in selling the center to the federal government in 1934. See Folders 1917 and 1935, NUC.

24 · Shivery, "History of Organized Social Work among Negroes in Atlanta," pp. 44–46, 60.

25 · Ibid., pp. 72–73.

26 · Minutes of Meetings of the Board of Directors, September 9, 1909, NUC; Shivery, "History of Organized Social Work among Negroes in Atlanta," p. 130.

27 · Shivery, "History of Organized Social Work among Negroes in Atlanta," p. 82.

28 · "Supplementary Report," undated folder, NUC.

29 · Undated materials, NUC.

30 · Shivery, "History of Organized Social Work among Negroes in Atlanta," pp. 52, 115–17. Four additional clinics were opened: White's Alley, Rock Street, Mount Olive Baptist Church, and Blanton's Hall.

31 · "Types of Services," New Document Folder (1934), NUC. For an examination of the purchase of the union property and development of the University Housing Project, see the minutes of May 11, July 17, and August 2, 1934; and February 12, March 12, April 9 and 19, May 12, July 8 and 19, and October 18, 1935. For an overall examination of the University Housing and Techwood Homes, see Michael L. Porter, "The Development and Amelioration of Housing Conditions in the Techwood Housing Area (1890–1938) and the University Housing Area (1930–1950)" (M.A. thesis, Atlanta University, 1972).

32 · Neighborhood Union Report, Folder 1913–1914, NUC. The

women on this committee were not all members of the union, but they were leading Black women of the city.

33 · Neighborhood Union Report, Folder 1914, NUC; "Survey of Colored Public Schools (1913–1914)," NUC; "Tenth Annual Report of the Women's Civic and Social Improvement Committee," NUC.

34 · Petition of the Women's Civic and Social Improvement Committee, August 19, 1913, NUC.

35 · "Tenth Annual Report," NUC.

36 · Shivery, "History of Organized Social Work among Negroes in Atlanta," pp. 101–2.

37 · Ibid., pp. 103–5. See also Bacote, "The Negro in Atlanta Politics," p. 342.

38 · Even with the approval of the new bond, accommodations were still inadequate for Black students. In September 1923, summarizing its second school survey in a letter to the mayor and City Council, the union reported: "The City has 17,750 Negro children, 34% of the school population. For the instruction of these children, there are twelve public school buildings. These have a total seating capacity of 4,877. The total enrollment is 11,469. Therefore, the seating capacity is only 43% of the total enrollment. The children are on triple session, and many children are on two and one half hour school sessions. Including the half-day teachers, there are 159 teachers for these 11,469 pupils, or an average of 72 children for each teacher employed. Only 203 pupils in the entire system are getting adequate school work, or less than 2% of the total" (Folder 1923, NUC).

39 · Walter Chivers, "Survey of Work of the Neighborhood Union," Folder 1923, NUC.

40 · "Atlanta Health Campaign," June 12, 1914. NUC.

41 · "Anti-Tuberculosis Campaign among Negroes Is Discussed," Atlanta *Constitution,* June 21, 1914, p. 1; Atlanta Anti-Tuberculosis Association, Annual Reports, 1916–1919, Colored Department, NUC; Shivery, "History of Organized Social Work among Negroes in Atlanta," pp. 21–22.

42 · "Partial Report of the Work of the Neighborhood Union to the Atlanta Tuberculosis Association for 1917, 1918, 1919," Colored Department, NUC; Shivery, "History of Organized Social Work among Negroes in Atlanta," pp. 165–66.

43 · Atlanta Anti-Tuberculosis Association, Annual Report, 1919, Col-

ored Department, NUC; Shivery, "History of Organized Social Work among Negroes in Atlanta," pp. 53, 131.

44 · Shivery, "History of Organized Social Work among Negroes in Atlanta," p. 53.

45 · Ibid., p. 240. See also "History of Social Service Institute," NUC.

46 · Atlanta School of Social Service, *Announcement of Atlanta School of Social Service at Morehouse College, Atlanta, Georgia* (pamphlet), 1920, NUC.

47 · Ibid; Atlanta School of Social Work, *Bulletin 1931–1932* (pamphlet), NUC.

48 · Shivery, "History of Organized Social Work among Negroes in Atlanta," pp. 107, 187–88. It should also be noted that at the beginning of September, Morehouse held its second Social Service Institute. Subjects discussed were the value of social service training, juvenile delinquency, training health in the schools, a survey of urban conditions in Atlanta, malnutrition, influence of music in the home, and infant care. Faculty members were generally the same as listed for the first institute. During evening sessions a film on health was shown. Enrollment was limited, and the fee was twenty-five cents. For further discussion see Clarence A. Bacote, *The Story of Atlanta University: A Century of Service* (Atlanta: Atlanta University Press, 1969).

49 · Shivery, "History of Organized Social Work among Negroes in Atlanta," pp. 290–96, 497–506.

50 · Telegram from Herbert Hoover to Lugenia Hope, May 28, 1927, Folder 1927, NUC; "Preliminary Report of a Committee Representing the Colored Advisory Commission of the Mississippi Valley Flood Relief on Rescue and Relief Assistance and Rehabilitation among Colored Flood Sufferers," Folders 1928 and 1935, NUC.

51 · Shivery, "History of Organized Social Work among Negroes in Atlanta," p. 498.

52 · Ibid., p. 505.

53 · "Report of the Emergency Committee of the Neighborhood Union," Folder 1935, NUC.

54 · Atlanta *Daily World,* July 8, 1933, p. 1; "A Tribute of Love and Appreciation to Lugenia Hope, Honoring Her on the Twenty-Fifth Anniversary of the Founding of the Neighborhood Union," Folder 1933, NUC; "Talk at the Testimonial Dinner Tendered Mrs. Lugenia Hope by

the Citizen's Committee, during the 25th Anniversary of the Neighborhood Union," Spelman College, July 11, 1933, NUC.

55 · Letter from Lugenia Hope to the Neighborhood Union, July 8, 1935, Folder 1935, NUC; Minutes of Meetings of the Board of Directors, July 19, 1935, NUC.

56 · Neighborhood Union Constitution, as revised in 1924, Folder 1924–1925, NUC.

57 · Edgar A. Guest, "The House by the Side of the Road," in Clinton T. Howell (ed.), *Better Than Gold* (Nashville: Thomas Nelson, 1970), p. 130.

Chapter Five

1 · The desire of white participants was to improve the lot of the Black community within the segregated society, not to abolish the structure of society. For example, in 1925 various interracial committees in Atlanta sponsored a concert by Black singer Roland Hayes. The sponsors realized that they would have to segregate the audience, so they divided the city auditorium down the middle. One entrance was used for both groups. Although white CIC members were proud of their efforts—over five thousand people attended without incident—John Hope reminded them that Blacks were as opposed in principle to horizontally segregated seats as they were to the regular segregated seating in the balcony. See *Atlanta Independent*, December 24, 1925; "Report of Mr. Clark Foreman at Meeting of the Georgia CIC (1926)," Commission on Interracial Cooperation Papers (hereafter cited as CIC Papers), Atlanta University Center-Woodruff Library; Ann Wells Ellis, "A Crusade Against Wretched Attitudes: The Commission on Interracial Cooperation's Activities in Atlanta," *Atlanta Historical Journal* 23 (Spring 1979): 27.

2 · Gladys G. Calkins, "The Negro in the Young Women's Christian Association: A Study of the Development of YWCA Interracial Policies and Practices in Their Historical Setting" (M.A. thesis, George Washington University, 1960), pp. 38–40.

3 · Ibid., pp. 40–41.

4 · Ibid., p. 42.

5 · Ibid., p. 43; Suggestions from the Committee on Findings at the

Conference on Colored Work, Louisville, Ky., October 14 and 16, 1915, CIC Papers.

6 · "June 1918: War Work among Colored Girls and Women," YWCA Folder, NUC; Jacquelyn D. Hall, *Revolt against Chivalry: Jessie Daniel Ames and the Women's Campaign against Lynching* (New York: Columbia University Press, 1979), p. 84; Giddings, *When and Where I Enter*, pp. 155–56.

7 · "War Work of Women's Council of Colored Women, Atlanta, Georgia," Folder 1917, NUC; "Minutes of Meeting Called by Neighborhood Union, Atlanta Colored Women's War Council to the Atlanta Division of the War Department Commission on Training Camp Activities," Folder 1918, NUC; Hall, *Revolt against Chivalry*, p. 287.

8 · "YWCA Colored American Women in War Work Issued by the Committee on Work among Colored Girls and Women of the War Work Council," YWCA Folder, NUC; Eva Bowles to Mrs. John Hope, July 30 and December 18, 1917, ibid.; "Report of Mrs. L. E. [sic] Hope, Camp Upton, L.I.," July 18, 1918, ibid.

9 · Minutes from an untitled meeting, undated, NUC; Giddings, *When and Where I Enter*, p. 156.

10 · Minutes from an untitled meeting, undated, NUC.

11 · Hall, *Revolt against Chivalry*, pp. 85, 287; Giddings, *When and Where I Enter*, p. 157.

12 · Minutes of Conference, undated, YWCA Folder, NUC.

13 · Ibid.

14 · Minutes from an untitled meeting, undated, NUC; Catherine D. Lealtad to Lugenia B. Hope, March 5, 1920, NUC.

15 · Minutes of Conference, undated, YWCA Folder, NUC.

16 · Shivery, "History of Organized Social Work among Atlanta Negroes," pp. 183–86.

17 · "Mrs. Hope on the Cleveland Meeting," May 20, 1920, YWCA Folder, NUC. See also Janie Porter Barrett to Lugenia Hope, February 8, 1921, ibid.

18 · "Mrs. Hope on the Cleveland Meeting," February 8, 1921, ibid.; Mary J. McCrorey to Lugenia B. Hope, May 7, 1920, ibid.

19 · Mary J. McCrorey to Lugenia B. Hope, May 7, 1920, ibid.

20 · "Minutes of the Meeting Held in Offices of the South Atlantic Field Committee, Richmond, Virginia, July 3, 1920, to Consider the Administration of Colored Work," ibid.

21 · Ibid.; Porter, "Black Atlanta," p. 85.

22 · "Minutes of the Meeting Held in Offices of the South Atlantic Field Committee," YWCA Folder, NUC; Mary J. McCrorey to Lugenia Hope, January 27, 1921, ibid. See also Lugenia Hope to Katherine Hawes, August 4, 1920, ibid.

23 · See Bishop J. S. Flipper, AME church, Atlanta, in the Cleveland *Advocate,* undated, ibid.; and an editorial in the *Advocate,* April 24, 1920, ibid.

24 · "Conference of Young Women's Christian Association on Colored Work," Louisville, Ky., February 25–27, 1921, ibid.; Ruth [?] to Lugenia Burns Hope, November 3, 1921, ibid.; Eva Bowles to Lugenia Hope, March 15, 1921, ibid.; Mrs. Lewis H. Lapham to Charlotte H. Brown, June 21, 1921, ibid.; Hall, *Revolt against Chivalry,* p. 86. Hall maintained that Lugenia had expected to receive the appointment offered to Brown. However, as vocal as Lugenia was in the various conferences against the YWCA's policies regarding Blacks, and as determined as she was to bring equity, parity, and independence to Black branches, it seems most unlikely that the National Board would have seriously considered her for membership or that she would have seriously expected to be considered.

25 · "Colored Women and the YWCA: A Statement of Policy," YWCA Folder, NUC. See also Louisville Conference, 1915, ibid.; and Richmond Conference, July 1920, ibid.

26 · Lugenia B. Hope to Eva D. Bowles, March 15, 1922, ibid.

27 · Mary J. McCrorey to Lugenia Hope, July 6, 1931, CIC Folder, NUC.

28 · Hall, *Revolt against Chivalry,* pp. 86–87.

29 · "Interracial Origin of Women's Group," CIC Folder, NUC.

30 · Ibid., Hall, *Revolt against Chivalry,* p. 89; Wilma Dykeman and James Stokely, *Seeds of Southern Change: The Life of Will Alexander* (Chicago: University of Chicago Press, 1962), pp. 89, 289.

31 · "Southern Negro Women on Race Co-Operation," CIC Folder, NUC; Ann Wells Ellis, "The Commission on Interracial Cooperation, 1919–1944: Its Activities and Results" (Ph.D. dissertation, Georgia State University, 1975), p. 29.

32 · Ellis, "The Commission on Interracial Cooperation," p. 30.

33 · Hall, *Revolt against Chivalry,* pp. 89–90.

34 · Concerning Jennie Moton, Lugenia wrote Marion Wilkinson: "Mrs. Moton (weak, very weak), well she is invited as company for Mrs. Washington, not to speak, however. I consider that more dangerous since

she will talk with every person who will talk to her. Of course you know that she is too compromising in her attitude on race relationship." September 19, 1920, CIC Folder, NUC.

35 · "Memphis Conference," CIC Papers.

36 · Ellis, "The Commission on Interracial Cooperation," p. 29.

37 · Charlotte Hawkins Brown, "Some Incidents in the Life and Career of Charlotte Hawkins Brown Growing out of Racial Situations, at the request of Dr. Ralph Bunche," Charlotte Hawkins Brown Papers (hereafter cited as CHB Papers), Schlesinger Library, Radcliffe College; Lugenia Hope to Mrs. Archibald Davis, March 1, 1921, CIC Folder, NUC.

38 · Mrs. Booker T. Washington to Lugenia Hope, November 15, 1920, CIC Folder, NUC. See also Giddings, *When and Where I Enter,* pp. 170–76; and Hall, *Revolt against Chivalry,* pp. 86, 127.

39 · Ellis, "The Commission on Interracial Cooperation," pp. 30–31. See also Lugenia Hope to Mrs. Archibald Davis, March 1, 1921, CIC Folder, NUC; Janie P. Barrett to Lugenia Hope, April 2, 1921, ibid.; and Carrie Parks Johnson to Lugenia Hope, February 13, 1921, and March 12, 1927, ibid.

40 · Minutes Continuation Committee, CIC Papers.

41 · Hall, *Revolt against Chivalry,* p. 97. See also Giddings, *When and Where I Enter,* pp. 172–76. This was not the end of the Black women's statement. The Southeastern Federation of Colored Women's Clubs, determined to inform the public about the position of southern Black women, adopted the statement as the federation platform and published it as a pamphlet under the title *Southern Negro Women and Race Co-operation.* The pamphlet omitted the controversial preamble, retained the suffrage plank, and adopted a conciliatory tone in its discussion of lynching.

42 · Minutes, Joint Meeting, Woman's General Committee and Interracial Committee of the Southeastern Federation of Colored Women's Clubs, October 20–21, 1922, CIC Folder, NUC. The Black women nominated and elected were Bethune, Wilkinson, Moton, McCrorey, Brown, Washington, and Lugenia. In 1925, when Washington died, Maggie L. Walker of Richmond, Va., replaced her.

43 · High Points from Minutes, Annual Meeting, Woman's General Committee, November 29, 1928, CIC Papers; Susan M. Nelson, "Association of Southern Women for the Prevention of Lynching and the Fel-

lowship of the Concerned: Southern Women and Racial Politics" (M.A. thesis, Emory University, 1982), p. 29.

44 · Robert B. Eleazar, "Southern Women against the Mob," *Southern Workman* 59 (March 1931): 126–31; Minutes from Annual Meeting, Woman's General Committee of CIC, November 19, 1928, Association of Southern Women for the Prevention of Lynching Papers (hereafter cited as ASWPL Papers), Atlanta University Center—Woodruff Library; Mrs. Booker T. Washington to Mrs. John Hope, September 22, 1922, CIC Folder, NUC.

45 · Ellis, "The Commission on Interracial Cooperation," p. 50.

46 · Nelson, "Association of Southern Women for the Prevention of Lynching," pp. 33, 36–37; Henry E. Barber, "The Association of Southern Women for the Prevention of Lynching, 1930–1942," *Phylon* 34 (December 1973): 378; Giddings, *When and Where I Enter*, pp. 207–9; Hall, *Revolt against Chivalry*, pp. 111–13.

47 · Nelson, "Association of Southern Women for the Prevention of Lynching," pp. 43–44; "Beginning of the Movement," 1932, ASWPL Papers.

48 · Edward F. Burrows, "The Commission on Interracial Cooperation, 1919–1944: A Case Study in the History of Interracial Movement in the South" (Ph.D. dissertation, University of Wisconsin, 1955), pp. 224, 383.

49 · Hall, *Revolt against Chivalry*, pp. 243–44; Giddings, *When and Where I Enter*, pp. 209–10.

50 · Minutes, ASWPL Annual Meeting, January 11, 1935, ASWPL Papers. Quoted also in Gerda Lerner, *Black Women in White America* (New York: Pantheon Books, 1972), pp. 473–77; Hall, *Revolt against Chivalry*, p. 244; and Giddings, *When and Where I Enter*, p. 210.

51 · Minutes, ASWPL Annual Meeting, January 11, 1935, ASWPL Papers.

52 · Eugena K. Jones to Mrs. John Hope, May 15, 1915, and May 26, 1916, undated folder, NUC; Shivery, "History of Organized Social Work among Negroes in Atlanta," chaps. for the years 1917–20.

53 · "Annual Report of the Secretary of the Atlanta Branch of the NAACP," January 1, 1935, NAACP Branch Files, January–December 1935, NAACP Papers, Manuscript Division, Library of Congress.

54 · Ibid., p. 4; NAACP, Atlanta Branch, Citizenship Committee, *A*

Primer on Citizenship Prepared and Used by Citizenship Training School (Atlanta, Ga.), 1933, NAACP Papers. The national office gave the Madame Walker Merit Award annually to the most outstanding and dedicated NAACP worker. In 1934 President Walden, along with some members of the Atlanta branch, submitted his name for consideration. But other local people felt that Walden's interests and energies were divided into too many directions and dismissed him as a "prestige-glory seeker" ("Annual Report of the Secretary of the Atlanta Branch of the NAACP," January 1, 1935, NAACP Papers). The Woman's Auxiliary severed its ties with the local branch in 1935. Its director wrote Roy Wilkins, the executive director, that in her judgment Lugenia was essentially responsible for the success of the citizenship schools; she believed, however, that Lugenia would be too modest to accept the award and would prefer to have it go to Logan. To resolve this explosive dilemma, President Walden was persuaded to step aside in return for election to the NAACP Board of Directors. See memorandum from Wilkins to Walter White, January 23, 1936, NAACP Papers; Josie Murphy to Walter White, May 31 and July 30, 1934, ibid.; Rosa M. Cosby to Dean William Pickens, May 30, 1934, ibid.; and Eugene Jones to Mr. W. F. White, March 11, 1936, ibid.

55 · "Annual Report of the Secretary of the Atlanta Branch of the NAACP," January 1, 1935, ibid.

Chapter Six

1 · Document on the funeral arrangements of John Hope, undated folder, Florence M. Read Correspondence Papers (hereafter cited as FMRCP), Atlanta University Center-Woodruff Library; family Bible of James and Ophelia Burns Bryant, in the possession of their granddaughter, Henrietta Bryant Daily Meredith, Chicago, Ill. Lugenia's mother died in 1917. She had maintained her fiscal responsibility to her mother and she visited her in Chicago periodically, but Mrs. Burns rarely visited Lugenia.

2 · Edward Hope, "My Mother," p. 9; personal notes of Lugenia Burns Hope, untitled, undated, Hope Folder, LLC.

3 · Personal interview with Dr. Clarence A. Bacote, Morehouse College, Atlanta, April 7, 1980.

4 · Executive Memorandum No. 34, July 10, 1941, Hope Folder, LLC;

Aunt Genie to Lloyd [Lewis], April 5, 1938, ibid.; L. B. Hope to Earle [Burns], May 15, 1938, ibid.

5 · On January 26, 1951, the National Association of Colored Graduate Nurses merged with the American Nurses Association; after seventeen years of activity, the former group was officially dissolved. See Mabel Keaton Staupers, *No Time for Prejudice: A Story of the Integration of Negroes in Nursing in the United States* (New York: Macmillan Co., 1961), pp. 68–97; and Mabel Keaton Staupers Papers, Moorland-Spingarn Research Center, Howard University.

6 · Mary McLeod Bethune to Lugenia Burns Hope, September 18, 1942, Black Women's National Archives, Washington, D.C.

7 · Florence Read to Dean Sage, April 18, 1943, FMRCP; Dean Sage to Lugenia B. Hope, April 20, 1943, FMRCP. John Hope III died in 1985, leaving a son, John Birnie Hope.

8 · Personal notes of Lugenia Hope, 1943, untitled, Hope Folder, LLC.

9 · Personal interviews with Henrietta Meredith, Chicago, Atlanta, and Macon, Ga., 1980–83; personal interview with Anna Elder, Chicago, March 19 and July 29–31, 1982; Marion C. Hope Papers, Anacostia Neighborhood Museum, Smithsonian Institution. Marion Hope was a notable social worker in Washington, D.C., whose activism almost duplicated her mother-in-law's. She was one of the founders of the Anacostia Neighborhood Museum, housing it in the beginning years in one of her own homes. When she died in 1974, her ashes were thrown over the Anacostia River in southwest Washington, where she lived and worked.

10 · "Biographical Statement of Mrs. John Hope," NUC.

11 · "Memorial Services in Honor of Mrs. Lugenia Burns Hope," Personal Folder, NUC; Atlanta University *Bulletin,* December 1947, p. 26; and Morehouse *Alumnus,* March–April 1948.

12 · Personal notes of Lugenia Burns Hope, Biographical Folder, JLBH.

Chapter Seven

1 · The title of this chapter comes from a speech by Nannie Helen Burroughs, published as "Not Color but Character" in *Voice of the People,* July 1904, pp. 277–79.

2 · Though many affluent Black women were very active in their struggle for racial betterment, this was not always the case. Some used their

positions and financial security for personal gain or individual mobility. Others, many of them mulattoes, merely used their "hues" to ease their accommodation and eventual assimilation into mainstream America. Yet some of the social activists were elitists who felt a strong sense of noblesse oblige. The point remains that their involvement, regardless of the degree, was an option they had, the result of personal commitment rather than something dictated by circumstances.

3 · See untitled, undated speech of Lugenia Burns Hope, Hope Folder, LLC.

4 · Jill Conway, "Women Reformers and American Culture, 1870–1930," In Jean Friedman and William Shade (eds.), *Our American Sisters: Women in American Life and Thought* (Lexington, Mass.: D. C. Heath and Co., 1982), pp. 432–41. See also Blanche W. Cook, "Female Support Networks and Political Activism: Lillian Wald, Crystal Eastman, Emma Goldman," in Linda K. Kerber and Jane DeHart Matthews (eds.), *Women's America: Refocusing the Past* (New York: Oxford University Press, 1982), pp. 274–93; Ray Ginger, "The Women of Hull House," in ibid, pp. 263–73; Allen F. Davis, *Spearheads for Reform: The Social Settlements and the Progressive Movement, 1890–1914* (New York: Oxford University Press, 1967); Jane Addams, *Twenty Years at Hull House* (1910; New York: Macmillan Co., 1938); and Lillian Ward, *The House on Henry Street* (New York, 1915).

5 · Charlotte Hawkins Brown's eulogy of Mrs. John Hope, CHB Papers.

6 · Mary McLeod Bethune, "Tribute to the Twenty-Fifth Anniversary of the Neighborhood Union," NUC.

Bibliography

Primary Sources

Manuscript Collections

The John and Lugenia Burns Hope Papers (Atlanta University Center)—Woodruff Library—contain mainly the works of John Hope. However, there are letters to Lugenia Burns Hope from John Hope, written as he traveled around the world, as well as a substantial number of love letters written before and after their marriage. There are also notes on her early years in Chicago and her beginning years in Atlanta.

The Neighborhood Union Collection (Atlanta University Center—Woodruff Library) proved to be the essential manuscript source for this study. These papers not only cover the planning, establishment, and organization of the Neighborhood Union but also include materials on Lugenia's personal life and her work with the Young Women's Christian Association (YWCA), the Commission on Interracial Cooperation (CIC), the Association of Southern Women for the Prevention of Lynching (ASWPL), the National Association of Colored Women (NACW), and the International Council of Women of the Darker Races.

The Lloyd Lewis Collection (Manuscript Division, University of Illinois, Chicago Circle Campus) proved invaluable in developing Lugenia's paternal and maternal lineages. Lloyd and Emma preserved many of Lugenia's notes and family photographs.

Other family papers were valuable for grasping the overall picture of the woman. These include the Marion C. Hope Papers (Anacostia Neighborhood Museum, Smithsonian Institution) and the John Hope II Papers (Amistad Collection, New Orleans).

The National Association for the Advancement of Colored People (NAACP) Papers (Manuscript Division, Library of Congress) contains the Atlanta branch papers, which deal with Lugenia's role in establishing citizenship schools in Atlanta during the 1930s.

Bibliography

The ASWPL Papers (Atlanta University Center—Woodruff Library) and the CIC Papers (Atlanta University Center—Woodruff Library) also document Lugenia's role in interracial work in the South. In addition to adding information on Lugenia, these papers cover the network of southern Black women who made up the core of the Southeastern Federation of Colored Women's Clubs, showing their importance to the interracial movement. Papers of Lugenia's contemporaries also provide a wealth of information on the Black clubwomen's movement.

The Mary McLeod Bethune Papers (Black Women's National Archives, Washington, D.C.; Amistad Collection, New Orleans; and the personal collection of Donnie Bellamy, Regents' Professor of History, Fort Valley State College, Fort Valley, Ga.) document Lugenia's involvement with the National Council of Negro Women and her travels with Bethune on inspection tours for the Negro Affairs Division of the National Youth Administration.

The Charlotte Hawkins Brown Collection (Schlesinger Library, Radcliffe College) includes a survey of Lugenia's work with the YWCA and the development of Black branches in the South. Brown's speech at the memorial service for Lugenia is also available here.

The Nannie Helen Burroughs Papers (Manuscript Division, Library of Congress) cover the work of Black women on the CIC. There are numerous letters between Burroughs and Jessie Daniel Ames, founder of the ASWPL, once the Women's Division of the CIC. These letters contain interesting materials on the interracial work of Black and white southern women.

The Mabel Keaton Staupers Papers (Moorland-Spingarn Research Center, Howard University) cover the history of the National Association of Colored Graduate Nurses, which Lugenia served as a member of its National Advisory Board and as a consultant to Staupers.

The Margaret Murray Washington Papers (Manuscript Division, Library of Congress; and Tuskegee Institute) give a good overview of the way one southern Black educated woman worked to improve the plight of her less fortunate sisters. Several letters between her and Lugenia are included, particularly concerning the International Council of Women of the Darker Races, which Lugenia served as a committee chairperson.

The Mary Church Terrell Papers (Moorland-Spingarn Research Center, Howard University; and Manuscript Division, Library of Congress) contain valuable information on the NACW Clubs and the International Council of Women of the Darker Races. Terrell's papers provide very extensive coverage of the Black clubwomen's movement.

Bibliography

The Carter G. Woodson Papers (Manuscript Division, Library of Congress) include information on the International Council of Women of the Darker Races. The Robert R. Moton Papers (Tuskegee Institute) were also helpful. The Hopes and Motons were close personal friends, and Lugenia and John used the Motons' summer place in Capashonic, Va., as a retreat on many occasions. The Florence M. Read Correspondence Papers (Atlanta University Center-Woodruff Library) include letters to the Hopes during John's last years at Atlanta University. They also contain information on his funeral arrangements and the granite grave marker that was purchased at Lugenia's request.

Government Documents and Publications

The reports of the Bureau of the Census for 1870, 1880, and 1900 were instrumental in developing the Burnses' history.

The Records of the War Department (National Archives) include materials on the mistreatment of Black soldiers in Georgia camps, one of the projects of Black Atlanta women during World War I.

Marriage and death certificates from the Bureau of Vital Statistics (Chicago and Nashville) verified Lugenia's age and her parents' full names.

School board records for the Board of Education of the city of Atlanta, 1912–24, proved useful in developing the role played by Lugenia and the Neighborhood Union in improving the Black public school system.

City directories, codes, and municipal reports were also helpful in the study of Black urban life.

Newspapers and Periodicals

One Black Georgia weekly and a Black Atlanta weekly and daily were very helpful: respectively, the Savannah *Tribune* (1892–1900), the Atlanta *Independent* (1904–20), and the Atlanta *Daily World* (1933, 1947, 1967). Two other Black weeklies covered the Black women's club movement and organization: the Cleveland (Ohio) *Advocate* (1920) reported on Black women and the YWCA meetings; the Chicago *Defender* (1935–41) carried several articles on the Hopes.

White dailies for the most part limited their coverage of racial news during this era to reports of lynchings or Black crime. Periodically the Atlanta *Constitution* (1905–24) did endorse some of the programs of the Neighborhood Union. However, most coverage by the Atlanta *Journal* (1904–7, 1944), the Atlanta *Georgian* (1906), and the Atlanta *News* (1906) concentrated on negative aspects of Black life in Georgia.

In addition to weekly newspapers, Blacks published a number of periodicals. Helpful to this study were Max Berber's *Voice of the Negro* (1904–5), which carried a series of articles by Black women; *The Crisis: A Record of the Darker Races,* which carried a series on Black women, including Lugenia (1912–17); an annual publication, the *Negro Year Book: An Encyclopedia of the Negro* (1912–20), edited at Tuskegee by Monroe Work; and *Who's Who in Colored America* (1915–27).

The Atlanta University Center Publications and School Histories

The Atlanta University Publications, published by the university's press, were the product of original research by Atlanta University students and teachers, especially W. E. B. Du Bois, on the conditions of Black Americans. Most helpful to this study were *The Negro Artisan* (No. 7, 1902), *Economic Cooperation among Negro Americans* (No. 17, 1911), *Morality among Negroes in Cities* (No. 1, 1896), and *Social Betterment among Negro Americans* (No. 3, 1898).

School newspapers and pamphlets used included the Atlanta University *Bulletin* (December 1947), the Spelman *Messenger* (1916–26), and the Morehouse *Alumnus* (1936, 1947, and 1948).

Relevant school histories are Clarence A. Bacote, *The Story of Atlanta University: A Century of Service* (Atlanta: Atlanta University Press, 1969); Edward A. Jones, *A Candle in the Dark: A History of Morehouse College* (Valley Forge, Pa.: Judson Press, 1967); Benjamin Brawley, *The History of Morehouse College* (Atlanta: Morehouse College, 1917); Myron W. Adams, *History of Atlanta University* (Atlanta: Atlanta University Press, 1930); and Florence M. Read, *The Story of Spelman College* (Princeton, N.J.: Princeton University Press, 1961).

Autobiographies

A number of Blacks have written of their experiences living in Georgia. James Weldon Johnson, in *Along This Way* (New York: Viking Press, 1933), described his days as an undergraduate at Atlanta University. Walter White was born and educated in Atlanta, and in *A Man Called White* (New York:

Macmillan Co., 1948) he gave a firsthand account of the Atlanta race riot of 1906. Henry Hugh Proctor, the pastor of First Congregational Church for a number of years, discussed his work in race relations in Atlanta in *Between Black and White: Autobiographical Sketches* (1925; New York: Viking Press, 1948). W. E. B. Du Bois recalled his years as a professor at Atlanta University in *Dusk of Dawn: An Essay toward an Autobiography of a Race Concept* (New York: Harcourt, Brace and Co., 1940). Benjamin J. Davis recounted his growing up in Atlanta and his years at Morehouse in *Communist Councilman from Harlem: Autobiographical Notes Written in a Federal Penitentiary* (New York: International Publishers, 1969). Benjamin E. Mays recalled Atlanta as it was when he first arrived from South Carolina and his early years at Morehouse College in *Born to Rebel: An Autobiography* (New York: Charles Scribner's Sons, 1971). Angelo Herndon described Atlanta and his trial in Georgia in *Let Me Live* (New York: Random House, 1937). Jesse O. Thomas discussed Atlanta and the beginning of the Urban League there in *My Story in Black and White* (Hicksville, N.Y.: Exposition Press, 1967). Robert R. Moton dealt with conditions in the South in his autobiography, *Finding a Way Out* (New York: Doubleday, Page and Co., 1920).

Autobiographies of Black women that aid in determining the overall condition of Black women and their experiences include Mary Church Terrell, *A Colored Woman in a White World* (Washington, D.C.: National Association of Colored Women's Clubs, 1968); Ann Moody, *Coming of Age in Mississippi* (New York: Dell Publishing Co., 1968); Erma Calderon, *Erma* (New York: Random House, 1981); and Pauli Murray, *Proud Shoes: The Story of an American Family* (New York: Harper and Row, 1984).

Interviews

Conversations with family members, former colleagues, former students, and people associated with Atlanta's history were of inestimable value. Lugenia's sons, Edward S. Hope, Sr. (Cleveland), and John Hope II (Washington, D.C.), supported this project and shared with me their recollections of their mother. Henrietta D. Meredith (Chicago), Lugenia's grandniece, proved to be the family historian. Without her aid the Burnses' history would have been difficult to reconstruct. Through her assistance, I was introduced to other family members who offered their help. Anna Elder (Chicago) was married to the son of Lugenia's first cousin and was instrumental in explaining the Burns family. Elise Hope (Washington, D.C.) recalled her relationship with her mother-in-law and recounted several stories of Lugenia's gaiety. Jeanette R. Burns Garrett (Detroit), grandniece of Lugenia, shared with me the history of Charley Burns I and his descendants.

Mae Harvey and Vivian Beavers (Atlanta), both members of the Inquirers, recollected the club's history and Lugenia's involvement. Mae Harvey also recounted the history of the Gate City Free Kindergarten Association and Lugenia's role in its founding. The late Clarence A. Bacote (Atlanta) and Rayford Logan (Washington, D.C.) were two great supporters of this project. Both had worked with Lugenia in the citizenship schools of the NAACP. Melvin Watson (Atlanta), former student and best friend of John Hope II, recalled the days when the two young scholars studied together under the "watchful eye" of Lugenia. His stepmother, Hattie Watson, was secretary of the Neighborhood Union for many years, and he recalled some of the union's programs. Information from other interviews with former students and colleagues was taken from Anne Beard, "Mrs. John Hope: Community Builder in Atlanta, Georgia, 1900–1936" (M.A. thesis, Atlanta University, 1975).

Secondary Sources

Biographies

The primary biography for this study is Ridgely Torrence's *The Story of John Hope* (New York: Macmillan Co., 1948). Yet Torrence's book contains little about Lugenia's life and works. Will W. Alexander's "Profile of John Hope" in *Phylon* 8 (First Quarter 1947): 1–13 details John's role in the CIC but does not recount any of Lugenia's involvement with the organization. A good description of the attitudes of the Black middle class of the early twentieth century can be obtained from Eugene Levy's *James Weldon Johnson: Black Leader, Black Voice* (Chicago: University of Chicago Press, 1973). Charles Martin's *The Angelo Herndon Case and Southern Justice* (Baton Rouge: Louisiana State University Press, 1976) describes race relations in Georgia around 1920.

Since there was no preexisting biography of Lugenia, biographies of other Black women have proved valuable as models and for information. Louise D. Hutchinson's *Anna J. Cooper: A Voice from the South* (Washington, D.C.: Smithsonian Institution, 1981) is an account of the life of the principal of the old M Street High School in Washington, D.C., and her outstanding educational career. Dorothy Sterling has recounted the lives of three Black women, Ellen Craft, Ida B. Wells, and Mary Church Terrell, in *Black Foremothers* (New York: Feminist Press, 1979). Alfreda M. Duster has edited and completed the autobiography of her mother, Ida B. Wells Barnett, published as *Crusade for Justice: The Autobiography of Ida B. Wells* (Chicago: University of Chicago Press, 1970). Rackham Holt has written a laudatory account, *Mary McLeod Bethune* (New York: Doubleday, 1964), of the educator and clubwoman.

Articles

Black women. Several articles by or about Black women appeared in *Voice of the Negro* in 1904–5: Anna Jones, "A Century of Progress of American Colored Women," September 1905, pp. 692–94; Josephine Bruce, "What Has Education Done for Colored Women?" July 1904, pp. 294–98; Nannie Helen Burroughs, "Not Color but Character," July 1904, pp. 277–79; Addie Hunton, "Negro Womanhood Defended," July 1904, pp. 280–82; Josephine Silone-Yates, "The National Association of Colored Women," July 1904, pp. 283–87; Mrs. Booker T. Washington, "Social Improvement of the Plantation Women," July 1904, pp. 288–90; Mary Church Terrell, "The Progress of Colored Women," July 1904, pp. 291–94; Sylvanie F. Williams, "The Social Status of the Negro Women," July 1904, pp. 298–300; and Fannie Barrier Williams, "An Extension of the Conference Spirit," July 1904, pp. 300–303.

An account of the club movement of Black women is found in Gerda Lerner's "Early Community Work of Black Club Women," *Journal of Negro History* 59 (April 1974): 158–67. For reviews of the self-help programs of southern Black women, see Cynthia Neverdon-Morton's "Self-Help Programs as Educational Activities of Black Women in the South, 1895–1925: Focus on Four Key Areas," *Journal of Negro Education* 53 (Summer 1982): 207–21; and also Neverdon-Morton's "The Black Woman's Struggle for Equality in the South, 1895–1925," in Sharon Harley and Rosalyn Terborg-Penn (eds.), *Afro-American Woman* (New York: Kennikat Press, 1978), 43–57.

Other useful articles on Black women include Mary S. Hundley, "The Association of Colored Women," *Opportunity* 3 (June 1925): 132–41; Anna E. Murray, "The Negro Woman," *Southern Workman* 33 (April 1904): 72–84; Mary T. Blaurelt, "The Race Problem as Discussed by

Negro Women," *American Journal of Sociology* 6 (March 1901): 662–72;
Sharon Harley, "Black Women in a Southern City: Washington, D.C.,
1890–1920," in Joanne V. Hawks and Sheild L. Skemp (eds.), *Sex, Race,
and the Role of Women in the South* (Jackson: University Press of Mississippi, 1983), pp. 59–74; Dolores Janiewski, "Sisters under Their Skins:
Southern Working Women, 1880–1950," in ibid., pp. 13–36; and Deborah G. White, "The Lives of Slave Women," *Southern Exposure* 12 (Nov-
ember/December 1984): 32–39. An account of southern Black women
during World War I is the focus of William J. Breen, "Black Women and
the Great War: Mobilization and Reform in the South," *Journal of Southern
History* 44 (August 1978): 421–40.

    Sage: A Scholarly Journal on Black Women is a new publication devoted
to the history of Black women. Two other scholarly journals have devoted
special issues to the study of Black women's history: *Journal of Negro
Education* 53 (Summer 1982) and *Black Scholar* 12 (November/December
1981).

Georgia and the South. Several articles discuss some aspect of Black wom-
en's history in Atlanta and in the South overall. E. Franklin Frazier, "The
Neighborhood Union in Atlanta," *Southern Workman* 52 (September
1923): 437–42, and Louie D. Shivery, "The Neighborhood Union," *Phylon* 3 (1942): 149–62, cover the founding of and programs undertaken
by the Neighborhood Union. Henry H. Proctor's "The Atlanta Plan of
Inter-Racial Cooperation," *Southern Workman* 49 (January 1920): 52–67,
and Ann W. Ellis's "A Crusade against Wretched Attitudes: The Commission on Interracial Cooperation Activities in Atlanta," *Atlanta Historical
Journal* 23 (Spring 1979): 21–44, focus on the CIC in Atlanta.

    Articles on Georgia by Clarence A. Bacote contribute to an under-
standing of racial politics, reform, and Black life in Georgia. See "Some
Aspects of Negro Life in Georgia, 1880–1908," *Journal of Negro History*
43 (Winter 1958): 186–213; "The Negro in Atlanta Politics," *Phylon* 16
(Fourth Quarter 1955): 333–52; "William Finch, Negro Councilman,
and Political Activities in Atlanta during the Early Reconstruction," *Journal of Negro History* 40 (October 1955): 341–64; and "Negro Proscrip-
tions, Protest, and Proposed Solutions in Georgia, 1880–1908," *Journal
of Southern History* 25 (November 1959): 471–98. Other articles dealing
with the political aspect of Atlanta and Georgia are Clement C. Moseley,
"The Political Influence of the Ku Klux Klan in Georgia, 1915–1925,"

Bibliography

Georgia Historical Quarterly 57 (Summer 1973): 235–55; and Dewey W. Grantham, Jr., "Georgia Politics and the Disfranchisement of the Negro," Georgia Historical Quarterly 32 (Winter 1948): 1–21.
Discussion of class structure in Atlanta's Black community may be found in August Meier and David Lewis, "History of the Negro Upper Class in Atlanta, Georgia, 1890–1958," Journal of Negro Education 28 (Spring 1959): 128–39. Charles Crowe explores the similarities between violence and the reform spirit in "Race Violence and Social Reform: Origins of the Atlanta Riot of 1906," Journal of Negro History 53 (July 1968): 234–56, and "Racial Massacre in Atlanta, September 22, 1906," Journal of Negro History 54 (April 1969): 150–73. Segregation and the Black community are described in Gilbert T. Stephenson, "The Segregation of the White and Negro Races in the Cities," South Atlantic Quarterly 13 (Winter 1914): 1–18; and Roger L. Rice, "Residential Segregation by Law, 1910–1917," Journal of Southern History 34 (May 1968): 179–99.

Books

Texts on Black women's history have been a recent phenomenon. See Sharon Harley and Rosalyn Terborg-Penn (eds.), Afro-American Woman (New York: Kennikat Press, 1978); Paula Giddings, When and Where I Enter: The Impact of Black Women on Race and Sex in America (New York: William Morrow and Co., 1984); Jacqueline Jones, Labor of Love, Labor of Sorrow; Black Women, Work, and the Family from Slavery to the Present (New York: Basic Books, 1985); Deborah G. White, Ar'n't I a Woman? Female Slaves in the Plantation South (New York: W. W. Norton and Co., 1985); Angela Y. Davis, Women, Race and Class (New York: Random House, 1981); Gloria Hull, Patricia Bell Scott, and Barbara Smith, All the Women Are White, All the Blacks Are Men, but Some of Us Are Brave (New York: Feminist Press, 1982); Filomina C. Steady (ed.), The Black Woman Cross-Culturally (Cambridge, Mass.: Schenkman Co., 1982); Bell Hooks, Ain't I a Woman: Black Women and Feminism (Boston: South End Press, 1981); Dorothy Sterling (ed.), We Are Your Sisters: Black Women in the Nineteenth Century (New York: W. W. Norton and Co., 1984); and Jo Ann Gibson Robinson, The Montgomery Bus Boycott and the Women Who Started It (Knoxville: University of Tennessee Press, 1987). Gerda Lerner (ed.), Black Women in White America (New York: Pantheon Books, 1972), is an anthology of works and speeches by and about Black women. Bert J.

Loewenberg and Ruth Bogin (eds.), *Black Women in Nineteenth Century American Life: Their Words, Their Thoughts, Their Feelings* (University Park: Pennsylvania State University Press, 1976), surveys speeches by and histories of Black women from the 1800s to the turn of the century.

Early studies, some authored by Black women, on the history of the Black women's club movement, Black women and World War I, notable Black women, and the overall history of Black women include Sadie I. Daniel, *Women Builders* (Washington, D.C.: Associated Publishers, 1931); Monroe Majors, *Noted Negro Women: Their Triumphs and Activities* (1893; New York: Books for Libraries Press, 1971); N. F. Mossell, *The Work of the Afro-American Women* (1908; New York: Books for Libraries Press, 1969); Sylvia Dannett, *Profile of Negro Womanhood* vol. 1, (New York: Educational Heritage, 1964); Hallie Q. Brown (ed.), *Homespun Heroines and Women of Distinction* (1926; New York: Books for Libraries Press, 1971,); Elizabeth L. Davis, *Lifting As They Climb* (Washington, D.C.: National Association of Colored Women's Clubs, 1933); and Addie Hunton and Kathryn M. Johnson, *Two Colored Women with the American Expeditionary Forces* (Brooklyn: Brooklyn Eagle Press, 1920). An account of the founding of the Graduate Colored Nurses Association is found in Mabel Keaton Staupers, *No Time for Prejudice: A Story of the Integration of Negroes in Nursing in the United States* (New York: Macmillan Co., 1961). Lawson A. Scruggs, *Women of Distinction* (Raleigh, N.C.: L. A. Scruggs, 1893), and Benjamin Brawley, *Women of Achievement* (Chicago: Woman's American Baptist Home Mission Society, 1919), were two of the earliest books on Black women by Black men.

There are other books that include some valuable discussion of Black women. Wilson Moses, *The Golden Age of Black Nationalism, 1850–1925* (Westport, Conn.: Archon Books, 1978), devotes a chapter to Afro-American women's history. Edyth Ross (ed.), *Black Heritage in Social Welfare, 1860–1930* (Metuchen, N.J.: Scarecrow Press, 1978), includes a discussion of the development of the Neighborhood Union in Atlanta. Robert Allen, *Reluctant Reformers: The Impact of Racism on American Social Reform Movements* (Washington, D.C.: Howard University Press, 1974), devotes a discussion to woman suffrage and white supremacy. In *The Negro Vanguard* (New York: Rinehart, 1959), Richard Bardolph incorporates Black women into a study of Black leadership. W. E. B. Du Bois, *Darkwater: Voices from within the Veil* (1921; New York: Arno Press, 1969), includes an essay on the plight of Black women in the South. Other general histories of women that incorporate some discussion of Blacks are June So-chen, *Herstory* (New York: Alfred Publishing Co., 1974); Eleanor Flexner, *Century of Struggle: The Women's Rights Movement in the United States*, rev. ed. (Cambridge, Mass.: Harvard University Press, 1975); Aileen Kraditor, *The Ideas of the Woman Suffrage Movement, 1890–1920* (New York: Columbia University Press, 1965); Jacquelyn D. Hall, *Revolt against Chivalry: Jessie Daniel Ames and the Women's Campaign against Lynching* (New York: Columbia University Press, 1979); Joanne V. Hawks and Sheild L. Skemp (eds.), *Sex, Race, and the Role of Women in the South* (Jackson: University Press of Mississippi, 1983); and Anne F. Scott, *The Southern Lady: From Pedestal to Politics, 1830–1930* (Chicago: University of Chicago Press, 1970).

Studies concentrating on the city of Atlanta and its people include Franklin M. Garrett, *Atlanta and Environs: A Chronicle of Its People and Events*, vol. 2 (New York: Lewis Historical Publishing Co., 1954); Paul Miller (ed.), *Atlanta: Capital of the South* (New York: O. Durrell, 1949); Dan Durrett and Dana White, *An-Other Atlanta: The Black Heritage* (Atlanta: The History Group, 1975); and C. A. Mahan, *The People of Atlanta* (Atlanta, 1950). Studies concentrating on Black Georgia are John Dittmer, *Black Georgia in the Progressive Era, 1900–1920* (Urbana: University of Illinois Press, 1977); E. R. Carter, *The Black Side: A Partial History of the Business, Religious and Educational Side of the Negro in Atlanta, Georgia* (Atlanta: E. R. Carter, 1894); Asa H. Gordon, *The Georgia Negro* (Ann Arbor: Edward Brothers, 1937); and Robert E. Perdue, *The Negro in Savannah, 1865–1900* (Hicksville, N.Y.: Exposition Press, 1973).

For an understanding of the South of the late nineteenth and early twentieth centuries, several books are important: Robert Haws (ed.), *The Age of Segregation: Race Relations in South, 1890–1945* (Jackson: University Press of Mississippi, 1978; see especially Mary F. Berry, "Repression of Blacks in the South, 1890–1945: Enforcing the System of Segregation," pp. 28–45); C. Vann Woodward, *Origins of the New South, 1877–1913* (Baton Rouge: Louisiana State University Press, 1967), and *The Strange Career of Jim Crow* (New York: Oxford University Press, 1974); George B. Tindall, *The Emergence of the New South, 1913–1945* (Baton Rouge: Louisiana State University Press, 1967); and Paul Gaston, *The New South Creed* (New York: Alfred Knopf, 1970).

Texts on the Black experience include John Hope Franklin, *From Slavery to Freedom: A History of Negro Americans*, 6th ed. (New York: Alfred

Knopf, 1987); August Meier, *Negro Thought in America, 1880–1915* (Ann Arbor: University of Michigan Press, 1971); Rayford Logan, *The Betrayal of the Negro: From Rutherford B. Hayes to Woodrow Wilson* (New York: Collier Books, 1970); Robert Brisbane, *The Black Vanguard: Origins of the Negro Social Revolution, 1900–1960* (Valley Forge, Pa.: Judson Press, 1970); Allison Davis, and Burleigh B. and Mary R. Gardner, *Deep South* (Chicago: University of Chicago Press, 1941); Gunnar Myrdal, *An American Dilemma,* vol. 2 (New York: Harper and Brothers, 1973); Alton Hornsby, Jr. (ed.), *In the Cage: Eyewitness Accounts of the Freed Negro in Southern Society, 1877–1929* (Chicago: Quadrangle Books, 1971); and Arnold Taylor, *Travail and Triumph: Black Life and Culture in the South since the Civil War* (Westport, Conn.: Greenwood Press, 1977).

Four older studies that were used are J. L. Nicholas and William H. Crogman, *Progress of a Race; or, the Remarkable Advancement of the American Negro* (1929; New York: Negro Universities Press, 1969); G. F. Richings, *Evidence of Progress among Colored People* (1897; Chicago: Afro-American Press, 1969); D. W. Culp (ed.), *Twentieth Century Negro Literature* (1929; New York: Arno Press, 1969); and Clement Richardson (ed.), *The National Encyclopedia of the Colored Race,* 2 vols. (Montgomery: National Publishing Co., 1919). Other valuable sources for this study were Kenneth T. Jackson, *The Ku Klux Klan in the City, 1915–1930* (New York: Oxford University Press, 1967); Blaine A. Brownell, *The Urban Ethos in the South, 1920–1930* (Baton Rouge: Louisiana State University Press, 1975); Howard N. Rabinowitz, *Race Relations in the Urban South, 1865–1890* (New York: Oxford University Press, 1978); Wilma Dykeman and James Stokely, *Seeds of Southern Change: The Life of Will Alexander* (Chicago: University of Chicago Press, 1962); Ray Stannard Baker, *Following the Color Line: American-Negro Citizenship in the Progressive Era* (1908; New York: Harper Torchbooks, 1964); Jean Friedman and William Shade (eds.), *Our American Sisters: Women in American Life and Thought* (Lexington, Mass.: D. C. Heath and Co., 1982); Linda K. Kerber and Jane DeHart Matthews (eds.), *Women's America: Refocusing the Past* (New York: Oxford University Press, 1982); Jane Addams, *Twenty Years at Hull House* (New York: Macmillan Co., 1910); Allen F. Davis, *Spearheads for Reform: The Social Settlements and the Progressive Movement, 1890–1914* (New York: Oxford University Press, 1967); Lillian Ward, *The House on Henry Street* (New York, 1915); and Mamie Garvin Fields, *Lemon Swamp and Other Places: A Carolina Memoir* (New York: Free Press, 1983).

Bibliography

Theses and Dissertations

Over the years, in master's theses that study the political, religious, economic, educational, social, and civic life of Black Atlanta and Black Georgia, a wealth of information has come out of Atlanta University's History Department (under the chairmanship for over forty years of Clarence A. Bacote and then of Margaret Rowley), along with the departments of Afro-American Studies, Sociology, and Social Work. Particularly germane to my study are Anne Beard, "Mrs. John Hope: Community Builder in Atlanta, Georgia, 1900–1936" (1975), and Louie D. Shivery, "The History of Organized Social Work among Negroes in Atlanta, 1890–1935" (1936). Comradge L. Henton, "Heman Perry: Documentary Materials for the Life History of a Business Man" (1948), contains excellent source material on Black business in Atlanta. Other significant theses from Atlanta University are Jean L. Conyers, "The Negro Businesswoman in Atlanta, Georgia" (1967); Michael L. Porter, "The Development and Amelioration of Housing Conditions in the Techwood Housing Area (1890–1938) and the University Housing Area (1930–1950)" (1972); Jesse W. Blalock, "Social, Political, Economic Aspects of Race Relations in Atlanta from 1890–1908" (1969); Mabel Glover Logan, "A Developmental History of the Gate City Day Nursery Association, Atlanta, Georgia" (1955); Augustus Adair, "A Political History of the Negro in Atlanta, 1908–1953" (1955); Leon Hollinshed, "Political, Educational, and Economic Aspects of the Atlanta Negro, 1880–1895" (1949); Irene Johnson, "Some Factors Related to Participation in Voluntary Associations" (1952); Eula Jones, "Voluntary Associations in the Atlanta Community" (1952); Bernard West, "Black Atlanta: Struggle for Development, 1915–1925" (1972); Dorothy Slade, "The Evolution of Negro Areas in the City of Atlanta" (1946); David A. Russell, Jr., "The Institutional Church in Transition: A Study of the First Congregational Church of Atlanta, Georgia" (1971); John Calhoun, "Significant Aspects of Some Negro Leaders' Contribution to the Progress of Atlanta, Georgia" (1968); Gloriastene Thompson, "The Expansion of the Negro Community in Atlanta, Georgia from 1940–1958" (1959); Louise E. Torrence, "Social Activities of the Negro Church in Atlanta, Georgia" (1934); Tommie L. Pradd, "A Study of Neighborhood Clubs of the Atlanta Urban League" (1939); Bettye Collier Thomas, "Race Relations in Atlanta from 1877 through 1890 as Seen in a Critical Analysis of the Atlanta City Council Proceedings and Other Related Works" (1966); Eugene P. Walker,

Bibliography

"Attitudes toward Negroes as Reflected in the Atlanta Constitution, 1908–1918" (1969); Edward R. Rodriguez, "A Study of the Discrimination in Race and Color Current in the City of Atlanta" (1934); Dean Rowley, "George Alexander Towns: A Profile of His Atlanta University Experience, 1885–1929" (1975); Martha Stafford, "Interracial Progress as Illustrated by the Work of the Atlanta Tuberculosis Association" (1939); Leatrice Traylor, "Leaders in Voluntary Associations" (1952); Joe E. Dinkins, "Some Aspects of the Economic Life of Black Atlantans, 1880–1900" (1972); Merlissie Ross Middleton, "Residential Distribution of Members of an Urban Church" (1953); Geraldine J. Perry, "The Negro as a Political Factor in Georgia, 1896 to 1912" (1947); and Lois Johnson, "Voluntary Associations: A Study in Status Behavior" (1952).

Some master's theses from other universities also need to be mentioned here. Mildred C. Mullins, "Homefront Activities of Atlanta Women during World War I" (Emory University, 1947), though it offers very little coverage of the role of Black women, is useful for background. Susan M. Nelson, "Association of Southern Women for the Prevention of Lynching and the Fellowship of the Concerned: Southern Churchwomen and Racial Politics" (Emory University, 1982), discusses the development of the ASWPL and the contributions of churchwomen of the Southern Regional Council; Nelson does not, however, cover the role and influence of Black women in the programs of these two groups. Ralph Wardlaw, "Negro Suffrage in Georgia, 1867–1930" (University of Georgia, 1932), is a helpful though not a thorough study. Gladys G. Calkins, "The Negro in the Young Women's Christian Association: A Study of the Development of YWCA Interracial Policies and Practices in Their Historical Setting" (George Washington University, 1960), unfortunately does not give an accurate or complete picture of Black women and the YWCA. Glenn Weddington Rainey, "Race Riot in Atlanta in 1906" (Emory University, 1929), fails to address the Black community's suffering as a result of the riot; though this thesis is degrading in tone, it is a good example of the attitudes of many whites on race relations during this era. Some discussion of various Black settlement work is included in Anna Lavinia Branch, "Atlanta and the American Settlement House Movement" (Emory University, 1972).

A number of doctoral dissertations have been helpful in preparing this study. Of major assistance have been Clarence A. Bacote's "The Negro in Georgia Politics, 1880–1908" (University of Chicago, 1955), which provides excellent background materials and insights into the problems faced by Black Georgians at the turn of the century; and Michael L. Porter's "Black Atlanta: An Interdisciplinary Study of Blacks in the East Side of Atlanta, 1890–1930" (Emory University, 1974), a thorough and extensive study of Black Atlanta and its development. Other significant studies are Horace Calvin Wingo, "Race Relations in Georgia, 1872–1908" (University of Georgia, 1969); John M. Matthews, "Studies in Race Relations in Georgia, 1890–1930" (Duke University, 1970); Alton D. Jones, "Progressivism in Georgia, 1898–1918" (Emory University, 1963); Thomas H. Deaton, "Atlanta during the Progressive Era" (University of Georgia, 1969); Philip N. Racine, "Atlanta's Schools: A History of the Public School System, 1896–1955" (Emory University, 1969); Helen B. Gouldner, "The Organization Woman: Patterns of Friendship and Organizational Commitment" (UCLA, 1960); Richard J. Hopkins, "Patterns of Persistence and Occupational Mobility in a Southern City: Atlanta, 1870–1920" (Emory University, 1972); Sharon M. Mullis, "The Public Career of Grace Towns Hamilton, Urban Activist and Public Reformer" (Emory University, 1976); Tulia Hamilton, "The National Association of Colored Women, 1890–1920" (Emory University, 1978); Darlene Roth, "Patterns in Women's Organizations, Atlanta, Georgia, 1890–1940" (George Washington University, 1978); Eugene Watts, "Characteristics of Candidates in City Politics: The Atlanta Experience, 1865–1903" (Emory University, 1969); Edward F. Burrows, "The Commission on Interracial Cooperation, 1919–1944: A Case Study in the History of Interracial Movement in the South" (University of Wisconsin, 1955); Alexa B. Henderson, "A Twentieth Century Black Experience: The Atlanta Life Insurance Company, 1905–1975" (Georgia State University, 1975); Timothy J. Crimmins, "The Crystal Stair: A Study of the Effects of Class, Race, and Ethnicity on Secondary Education in Atlanta, 1872–1925" (Emory University, 1972); Maggie M. Gilead, "Reynoldstown: A Search for Community" (Emory University, 1981); and Ann Wells Ellis, "The Commission on Interracial Cooperation, 1919–1944: Its Activities and Results" (Georgia State University, 1975).

Index

Washington, Booker T., 134; John opposes, 28; lectures for Neighborhood Union, 79

Washington, Forrester B., 84

Washington, Margaret Murray, 55; and Tuskegee Woman's Club, 5, 8; lectures for Neighborhood Union, 69; dedicates new Health Center, 73; at NACW conference of 1920, 108, 109; efforts to form CIC women's division, 110, 112; works to institute Black history courses, 115

Watson, Tom, 41

Wells-Barnett, Ida, 14, 15, 18

Weltner, Phillip, 71

West Fair (Atlanta), 60–62; day-care centers in, 3; Atlanta Baptist College in, 26; children of, 29; and Atlanta University students, 50–51; Neighborhood Union in, 66, 87; conditions in, 67

White primaries, 57

Whites: control Black YWCA branches, 1–2; and working women, 6; and discrimination, 7–8; and interracial movement, 91; at NACW conference of 1920, 108–110

White, Walter, 42

White, Rev. William, 5

Williams, Rev. A. D., 78, 119

Wilkerson, Marion, 5, 100

Woman's American Baptist Home Mission Society, 72

Women: Southern Black, reform movement of, 4, 118, 130; working, 6, 58–59; convicts, 7; nineteenth-century, 8–9; Black, in interracial movement, 91; Black, and YWCA, 92–94, 96–107; attempt to form CIC division, 109–14; Black, oppression of, 110–11; and lynchings, 116

Women's General Committee, CIC, 114

Women's Missionary Council, 111

Woodson, Carter G., 115

World's Columbian Exposition (1893), 18

World War I: and YWCA reform efforts, 1, 94–96; Lugenia's work during, 3

Wright, Edward H., 14

Wynn, Ida, 28, 35

Young Women's Christian Association (YWCA): National Board, 1, 2, 92, 94, 97, 98, 100, 101–6; and Black branches, 1–2, 92–94; Black hostess-house program, 3, 53; World War I work, 94–96; efforts to integrate, 96–107